T0287463

UNITED

with DAD

U N I T E D
with DAD

by Simon Lloyd

First published by Pitch Publishing, 2023

Pitch Publishing
9 Donnington Park,
85 Birdham Road,
Chichester,
West Sussex,
PO20 7AJ
www.pitchpublishing.co.uk
info@pitchpublishing.co.uk

A CIP catalogue record is available for this book
from the British Library.

ISBN 978 1 80150 460 7

Typesetting and origination by Pitch Publishing
Printed and bound in India by Thomson Press

Contents

For Ethan, Robyn and Lauren.

For everything. I love you.

Introduction

THE OLDER I get, the more I question if I could have done without football. It hasn't quite reached the point where I *resent* it, but there are definitely times when I'll catch myself wondering what life might have been had it not been there, near constantly, swallowing up more hours and days and weekends than I'll ever be able to count. I'll think about how much happier I might have been had my mood not been tied to the fortunes of a football club that, if I'm being honest, values me only as a paying customer, not a fan.

I know, just as any supporter knows, that in the grand scheme of things football doesn't – or *shouldn't* – matter. This world is stuffed full of terrible things far worthier of keeping me up at night than an FA Cup fourth round defeat to Middlesbrough. Wars still happen. Kids still go to bed hungry. As a species, we're continuing to ignore all the warnings about scorching our planet to the brink of inhabitability. Why, then, when I know there are much bigger, much more important things to get worked up about, will I let the sight of James Ward-Prowse preparing to take a late corner in a delicately poised league game make me feel sick or send my pulse soaring to the extent that my heart might burst? It's pathetic that I've allowed myself to be so hopelessly consumed by it.

There are, though, occasions in your life which, whether you like it or not, leave a mark, that set you on a certain path and contribute to who you are and what does and doesn't matter. For me, my first visit to Old Trafford was one of those occasions.

Now, it would be great for the sake of a more enthralling start to this if I could reel off some romantic tale about the night I first saw Manchester United play. I wish I could tell you about how I was mesmerised by the scintillating attacking play or describe the feeling I felt when the Stretford End erupted after the first goal. But, disappointingly, I can't do that. I have no such stories to tell of what, with hindsight and a watch of some grainy YouTube footage, was very clearly a miserable and largely uneventful game of football.

It happened when I was seven, on a baltic November evening in 1993. It should have been a formality. United, having scratched their 26-year itch in winning the Premier League earlier that year, were rampant, winning eight league games on the spin and already looking good value to retain their crown. In contrast, their opponents were a struggling Ipswich Town side who had won just once since August and looked destined to be sucked into a relegation scrap in the months ahead. This, then, would surely be a routine United win. Even if they didn't click, they'd probably still have enough about them to win by two or three goals. It would be, as Dad had probably factored in beforehand, the ideal night to anoint me a fully fledged, match-going United supporter.

Except, no; it finished 0-0.

Save for Ryan Giggs clipping the top of a crossbar with a late free kick, I can't recall anything of the game itself. I doubt any of the other 40-odd thousand in attendance could, either. Other things, however, have stayed with me. I'll never forget, clichéd though it sounds, that sacred first view of the floodlit turf, nor the moment a man in front of us shouted 'fuck off' at the referee, then remembered there were children sitting behind him and quickly turned to offer an apology.

But nothing I witnessed that night comes quite so vividly as the brief exchange I had with Dad as we got back to the car after full time.

There had been the odd flurry of snow in the air as we left the ground. My breath had left my mouth in thick, misty clouds. Away from the warmth of the crowd, I'd started to shiver. Dad had parked on a small scrap of wasteland somewhere on Trafford Park, tucked away between a couple of tired-looking warehouses and a crumbling brick wall with shards of green and brown glass cemented along its top. Old Trafford – still a single-tiered bowl in those days – was hidden from view, the glow of the floodlights in the night sky above offering the only clue it lay so close. As he unlocked the car door I asked, teeth chattering, if this was it now – if we would be coming to the next game, then the one after that and so on. He had turned to me, smiling a smile I didn't understand.

'Would you like that,' he said, 'if we come to more games?'

'Yes,' I'd replied. The smile had widened. And that, I think, was probably the exact moment he knew. Yes, the game had been shit and I hadn't even seen a goal, yet there I was, shivering, tired, but wanting more.

Years later, as Dad lay slowly dying in a nursing home bed – cancer cells charging through his body, mind gradually forgetting nearly everyone and everything he'd ever known – I often thought of that night and his smile as we reached the car. I hated that, of all the things, it was this that repeatedly came to mind, but perhaps it was understandable. As is often the way with father-son relationships, ours was not always smooth and straightforward. We were, in many ways, very different people who clashed regularly – especially throughout my teenage years. United, though, was our common ground; the shared love that brought us together. Any disagreement between us could usually be set aside and forgotten for a couple of hours at the match.

Dad had fallen in love with United while watching them at Old Trafford as a boy in the mid-1950s. From there, right through to those agonising final months, his passion for the club never completely faded away even when so many other things did. His affection for United rubbed off on me along the way and, towards the end, in those increasingly rare moments of lucidity when the morphine seemed to be doing its job, it was all that remained between us: something I felt – and probably always will feel – both grateful for and guilty about in equal measure.

It's those feelings that have led here, to this book. *United with Dad* is, on the surface, about the final two years of my father's life, drawing on his and our memories watching Manchester United. The details are of course unique to my experience, but I hope there's something within these pages that might strike a chord with others who know what it is to devote a large chunk of their life to watching their team beside someone they love, then one day realise the time has come to go on doing so without them.

Chapter 1

Looking for Wayne

ON A rain-sodden Wednesday evening a couple of weeks before Christmas 2017, Dad and I watched Manchester United labour to an unconvincing 1-0 home win over Bournemouth – a game so unremarkable I would almost certainly have forgotten it quite quickly were it not for what happened.

The first drops of rain had fallen in the hour before kick-off as we crossed the footbridge over Salford Quays and we'd briefly contemplated nipping back to the car to get the knackered old golf umbrella, which stayed in the boot for emergencies. We decided to push on, quickly regretting the decision. As we reached the first of the street vendor stalls and heart-attack burger vans lining Wharfside Way, it was pissing it down, billowing in hard at near-sideways angles.

Old Trafford was in sight by then, rising up above the roof of the last of the warehouses on the fringes of Trafford Park, red neon lettering running across the top of the stands like a harbour lighthouse to ships seeking shelter from the squall. We pressed on towards it, heads down, hoods up – passing the besieged fanzine sellers and hi-viz-clad security staff, weaving between the crawling queues of traffic filtering into the car parks at the back of the Stretford End.

Dad hobbled along and I sympathetically kept to his pace, resisting the urge to break away from him and burst into a run for the last couple of hundred yards. Finally, we reached the large foyer at the foot of the Sir Alex Ferguson Stand, where we scanned our tickets and silently queued for the lift, small puddles forming on the tiled floor around our feet as we waited.

The conditions outside had perfectly captured the mood of the place. Only three days had passed since the last home game: a derby against City. United had lost it 2-1, allowing City to open up an 11-point lead at the top of the table. Even with over half a season still to play, the margin had felt depressingly unassailable. Losing to *them* was never enjoyable, but this one had been particularly chastening given how well the season had started.

After spluttering through much of José Mourinho's first year as manager, United, buoyed by their Europa League Final win over Ajax in Stockholm before the summer, had been consistently good in their first few domestic and Champions League games. City had matched their early form in the league, but that was something to worry about later. A sense of cautious optimism had grown among even the most grounded and sensible of United supporters – particularly after a cluster of 4-0 wins in August and September. For the first time since Fergie, they actually *looked* like a side capable of mounting a title challenge. And after the turbulence of the four years that had passed since his retirement, quelling the excitement was proving difficult.

It didn't last long. After their promising start, United stuttered after the first international break of the season. A draw with Liverpool at Anfield wasn't a terrible result, but a week later they turned in a wretched performance at newly promoted Huddersfield Town and were deservedly on the wrong end of a 2-1 scoreline. Another defeat had come away at Chelsea in early November.

On each of these three occasions City, hitting their stride in their second season under Pep Guardiola, won their games, suddenly opening up an ominous lead at the top of the table. The derby, then, had been must-win, a final chance to stop them slipping out of reach. Defeat had been a crushing, almost-certainly terminal blow as far as the title was concerned. The hope of those balmy late-summer afternoons at the start of the season felt far longer ago than just a matter of weeks.

Out of the lift, the weather and lingering disappointment from the weekend had sapped the concourse of the usual buzz of anticipation that comes with a midweek game under the floodlights. It was unmistakably flat – the kind of night when many in attendance might have quietly wondered if stopping in and watching from the couch might have been the better option.

Dad wiped his misted-up glasses with a crumpled tissue and made for the usual kiosk, digging out enough coins for a programme, which he rolled up and wedged into one of the pockets of his sensible waterproof coat. As he did, I said hello to Frank and Nigel and the other regulars, whose names I was never certain of, who gathered in the usual spot opposite the steps up to our seats.

Nigel, as usual, was at the centre of the pre-match discussion, questioning Mourinho's tactical approach in the derby. Nige came down to Manchester on a coach from somewhere up near Carlisle or Penrith for every game, sinking a few beers in a nearby pub in the hours before kick-off. He was a big bloke – easily over six feet – and probably in his late 50s. Nige was a popular figure in our block: funny, intelligent. For years, he'd sat in the row in front of us, always seeming to wear the same sun-faded baseball cap and heckling referees with an impressively wide range of expletive-laden insults. Frank was a bit older, probably just into his 70s, and more reserved. Like Dad, he'd first attended Old Trafford as a boy in the 1950s. Frank lived somewhere between Salford and

Bolton and, if I remember rightly, had used to come to games with his daughter for years before she had grown up and got married to someone who didn't support United. He was more reserved and not as vocal as Nige. Few were.

'Is he avoiding us again?' Frank had joked, nodding in the direction of the steps. I turned to see Dad making his way up, the only person in the ground who appeared in a hurry to take his seat 20 minutes before kick-off. I shrugged, relieved most of the group were too engrossed with Nige's Mourinho rant to notice.

By then, the feeling that something wasn't quite right had already been nagging me. Dad had been acting strangely for a while. How long, exactly, I couldn't be sure. Save for the odd birthday or Christmas dinner, going to the football was the only quality time we now spent together, so naturally it was on matchdays that I had gradually noticed the changes. I suspected others were also becoming aware of them, as Frank's quip suggested.

Avoiding the concourse chats with the others was only a part of it. I'd first become aware of it – whatever *it* was – during the run of 4-0 wins early in the season. He'd been unusually subdued in the immediate aftermath of the goals, remaining seated when everyone else instinctively leapt to their feet in celebration. Against Everton in September, when United scored three times in the last ten minutes, he'd barely stirred at all and even seemed mildly irritated by the fuss being made of the late glut of goals.

Whatever it was, I was fairly certain it wasn't the cancer. They'd said at his last hospital appointment that all was under control in that department, and so I convinced myself it was probably something not quite so serious. His arthritic right knee had bothered him for years and badly needed replacing. It had slowed what was once a 20-minute walk from car park to turnstile to a 45-minute hobble. On top of that, he'd had a mild heart attack 18 months earlier, meaning the stairs up to the second tier were now completely out of the question. Matchday and the physical toll it took for him just to reach the ground was becoming an obvious problem. Perhaps, I told myself, whatever was behind it was related to that in some way.

In an ideal world, I could have just asked him, but it wasn't so straightforward. A mix of pride and stereotypically bloke-ish stubbornness meant discussing these things openly with him was akin to drawing blood from a stone. As a young man, he'd played cricket and football at decent levels, continuing to do the latter at semi-pro until well into his 30s. He'd been a PE teacher, played golf regularly, hiked up God knows how many mountains in the Lake District and Swiss Alps. He prided himself on being physically fit. Admitting his body no longer worked in the way it once did was something he found difficult, even when he reached an age where it was expected.

A few months earlier, shortly after his season ticket renewal letter had landed on the doormat in the spring, my mum had gently put it to him that going to games so often might be unwise. Choosing her words carefully, she suggested the time had come to take it a bit easier and at least *consider* giving it up. He was having none of it and shut down the conversation before it became one. His renewal form was completed that same night and in the post the very next morning, as if to make a point.

Weeks later, as we walked along the quayside after the final home game of the 2016/17 season, sun on our faces, water beside us mirror-smooth, he'd assured me that matchdays weren't becoming too much. His knee, he insisted, was manageable and he suggested we left home earlier to allow for any extra time he needed to walk to the ground from the car. He assured me the steps up to our seats in the second tier of the Sir Alex Ferguson Stand wouldn't be an issue either; we'd be able to get the lift. Going to the football was something he'd always done; he wasn't yet ready to stay at home watching United from his comfy chair, dog snoozing at his feet. Crumbling knee joints and a dodgy ticker might have denied him the active lifestyle he'd once led, but he was determined to at least cling to that.

We'd broken up the walk back that day by stopping off for our traditional end-of-season pint at one of the bars near Media City. Taking a seat at a table outside, he had asked after my son, Ethan, who was four months old at the time and at home with my wife, Lauren. I took out my phone and showed him some of the latest pictures.

'When I've taken my grandson to his first game,' he said, smiling as I flicked my thumb across the screen, 'then I'll think about giving it up'.

'Not before then.'

I reached my seat just as the intro riff for 'This Is the One' by the Stone Roses rumbled through the stadium speakers. Dad was sitting down already, rolled-up programme still poking out from the top of his coat pocket. The players emerged from the tunnel, sheets of rain continuing to sweep in as they completed the obligatory pre-kick-off handshakes. Dad stood but opted not to join in the half-arsed cheers as the starting XIs were read out.

The match, much like the atmosphere, was predictably dull in the opening minutes. United were lethargic, looking every inch a team who'd just lost a crucial derby and felt a bit sorry for themselves. The schedule had afforded Bournemouth an extra day's rest since their last game – a point Mourinho would almost certainly have noted in his post-match press conference later on that night – and were sharper and more dangerous for it. They should have scored at least once early on but were thwarted by David de Gea.

Then, just as the crowd was beginning to grow restless midway through the half, Anthony Martial carried the ball down United's left, cut back and fed it infield to Juan Mata, 25 yards from goal. He glanced up, quickly shifted the ball on to his left foot and arced a cross towards the back post, where Romelu Lukaku had pulled into space between two defenders. Lukaku guided his header into the corner of the goal; United took an undeserved lead.

I don't think Dad cheered the goal but he did at least manage to stand and applaud on this occasion, albeit a couple of seconds after everyone else. After muttering something about the quality of the cross, he took his seat again.

He'd been quiet nearly all game, chipping in with the occasional tut or exasperated groan when a pass went astray. Then, in the lull which followed the brief spike in excitement for the Lukaku goal, he cleared his throat and leaned towards me, preparing to say something.

'Why's Rooney not playing tonight?' he asked, voice barely more than a whisper.

'What?' I replied, not sure if I'd misheard him or if this was an attempted joke that didn't land. 'Why isn't Rooney playing?' he repeated, slightly louder this time, irritated at having to ask again.

I froze, not really knowing how to react, conscious of a slight fluttering sensation somewhere in my stomach. Wayne Rooney *was* playing that night, just not at Old Trafford. Instead, as I would find out later, he was at St James' Park, where he scored a winning goal against Newcastle for Everton.

An awkward silence hung between us. Had anyone else heard him, I wondered. Nige, I suspected, had. I was aware that his head had half turned around – probably about to take the piss – before he abruptly stopped himself and spun back towards the pitch. Seconds passed. Consciously keeping my voice low so as not to draw extra attention, I reminded Dad that Rooney had returned to Everton in the summer. There was no response. His eyes remained fixed on the pitch, not really following the movement of the ball, and the game drifted on uneventfully towards the end of the first half.

Dad had loved watching Rooney, especially the unpredictable, streetfighter version he'd been when he first joined United – just as likely to chin someone or tell a referee to fuck off as he was smash a volley into the top corner. That unpredictability was part of the thrill in those early days.

Dad was always drawn to the players who could look after themselves physically: Duncan, Robson, Hughes, Keane. Rooney, even at a young age, fell into that bracket and quickly became the player he looked for first during the pre-match warm-ups to make sure he was playing.

Years ago, on the night of Rooney's debut – the Fenerbahçe game, where he scored the hat-trick – a work commitment had forced Dad to pass on his ticket to my younger brother, Chris. He'd watched most of the game on TV. After full time, as we queued at the back of the South Stand for a train away from the ground, Dad called my phone unexpectedly. He was nearby, he said, and could give us a lift home. This proved to be only half true. After we got into the car it emerged he hadn't been nearby at all, but had been so childishly excited by what he'd seen that he'd felt the need to make a special journey to pick us up, just so he could talk to us about Rooney for an extra half an hour before bed. 'What a player, eh?' had been his first words as I opened the passenger door. 'What a bloody player that lad is.'

The strange, uneasy feeling I experienced in the pit of my stomach when Dad had asked why Rooney wasn't playing slowly subsided. By the time he shuffled off down our row to beat the queues for the toilets just before half-time, I was satisfied it was probably nothing more than the sort of minor lapse plenty of people his age were occasionally prone to. It wasn't, of course, and I would realise this soon enough, but I was guilty of the kind of delusional thinking all football fans are cursed with. As a sport, it conditions us to hang on to a hope that things will turn out better than expected – even when all the evidence suggests that won't be the case. It's the same reason very few supporters head for the exits when they see their team go 3-0 down inside the first 20 minutes, or why people ever bother deciding to support Tottenham.

At half-time I remained in my seat as most in our block headed down below for a piss or to buy an overpriced plastic bottle of beer. The TV screens dotted around the concourse played the highlights for the first half on loop, but the football on show didn't really merit a second viewing. Dad had left his programme under his seat, so I flicked through it, then chatted to Frank about his plans for Christmas with the grandkids and a reasonably priced Mediterranean cruise he and his wife had booked for sometime the next year. Dave and his grandson Matty, who sat immediately behind us and came across from Wrexham for every home game, had explained how heavy snow had forced them to abandon their attempts to make the derby at the weekend. Dad returned just as the players reappeared from the tunnel and the second half begun.

United were marginally better to begin with but struggled to convert possession into decent chances. Marcus Rashford cracked a shot from distance against the crossbar, which was as close as they came to a second. Inevitably, having failed to kill Bournemouth off, United began to look more vulnerable as time ticked on. Jermain Defoe came on with 20 minutes remaining, glided past Phil Jones and drilled a shot into De Gea's shins from a tight angle. Bournemouth ran out of steam after that. United seemed to settle and find a measure of composure as the game entered the final ten minutes.

With Christmas on the horizon, a burst of '12 Cantonas' had floated over from the Stretford End and was taken up by a few of those in K Stand. And then, as the chant faded away, it happened.

Owed partly to the dreariness of the game, I assumed, Dad had been even quieter throughout the second half than he had in the first. He'd spent it hunched forward, elbows resting on his thighs, gloved fingers loosely interlocked. Slowly, he began to sit up, easing himself back in his seat.

Again, he cleared his throat. Again he leaned his head towards mine. And again, he asked, 'Why's Rooney not playing tonight?'

Oh shit, I thought.

Chapter 2

Duncan

DAD TOLD the story countless times: three days before his tenth birthday, my grandad told him over the breakfast table that they were going out for the afternoon and wouldn't be returning until early evening. He hadn't expanded on where they were going and refused to provide further details when Dad attempted to press him on it. 'You'll see,' he'd replied, continuing to read the newspaper.

The announcement confused Dad, particularly because it came on a Saturday morning. His parents had run the pub for several years by then. Saturday, he'd come to know, was the one day of the week where, without exception, his father simply *had* to work.

Shortly after midday, the pair of them had made the short walk to the station, where the platform had been more crowded than Dad had ever seen it, and boarded a train towards Manchester. Along with nearly all the other passengers, they disembarked a couple of stops down the line at Eccles, where a row of buses queued along the kerb at the station front.

My grandfather led Dad by the hand towards one of the buses and they climbed aboard. Only as it pulled away from the station did he finally reveal their destination: Old Trafford, where they would see Manchester United play a game of football. Dad couldn't believe his luck. Over the course of a series of months, he'd pleaded with his parents to go to a United match. Some of the older boys in his school had gone to Old Trafford on a regular basis and their tales of what it was like had fuelled his desire to go and see it all for himself. And so, on 20 March 1954, he stood in the United Road stand and watched on through the haze of tobacco smoke which hung above the crowd as United beat Huddersfield Town 3-1 – his first game.

He could never recall the goals from that afternoon but knew he'd been looking in the opposite direction when Jack Rowley had scored the first of them. He also remembered how, even with spring in the Manchester air, the pitch had been heavy and thick with mud, so much so that the players had struggled to stay upright or control the ball as the game went on. The playing surface became worse, especially in the second half, and the quality of football suffered badly as a consequence. One player, though, wearing United's number six shirt, had appeared completely unperturbed by the slippery, churned-up pitch and Dad was struck by his composure and the ease with which he coped with the conditions. While other players skidded around him, his balance and poise had seemed almost unnatural for such a powerfully built man – although 'man' wasn't technically the correct word.

Duncan Edwards was still six months shy of his 18th birthday on the day Dad first laid eyes on him. He had made his first appearances in United's first team before helping them win the FA Youth Cup at the end of the previous season. He would be part of the side which would retain the trophy later that year, then again 12 months after. Despite this starlet's tender years, Matt Busby had absolute faith in his ability to make the step up and had been so impressed by his seamless transition to the men's game that he was now appearing on a regular basis. Even then, it was abundantly clear he was something very special.

Dad had left Old Trafford that day knowing he wanted to return as soon as he possibly could, his passion for United ignited. He'd also learnt that the player in the number six shirt had been called 'Edwards', but that most people in the crowd around him only seemed to call him by his first name. The next week, when Dad and his friends scuffed a battered ball around the school yard at break time, he pretended to be Duncan for the first time.

Two years earlier, Edwards had arrived in Manchester as a painfully shy 15-year-old having been born and raised in Dudley in the West Midlands. United getting him was a big deal. At 13, he'd turned out for England Schoolboys in a game against Wales at Wembley. Local sides Wolverhampton Wanderers and Aston Villa were both keen to sign him and were understandably peeved to discover he'd opted to make the move north and join United.

His arrival came as part of a process which had been set in motion two decades earlier. Salford-born businessman James W. Gibson helped save United from the brink of financial oblivion in the 1930s, holding the position of chairman until he died in 1951. Dad had once shown me the circular red plaque carrying his name which is fixed to the railway bridge on Sir Matt Busby Way. Having injected an initial £2,000 to United's coffers on arrival, Gibson quickly identified the need for the club to produce its own players. So much of what United came to be in the years that followed can be traced back to his foresight.

United entered a youth side in the Manchester League in 1932 as a means of developing local boys who would one day be ready to serve the first team. Five years later, the Manchester United Junior Athletics Club – commonly abbreviated to MUJAC – was formed. It was a model which was ahead of its time, a precursor of the academies we see in the modern game. MUJAC operated throughout the Second World War, even though the first team were unable to. This proved crucial when the fighting was over, with newly appointed manager Matt Busby able to bolster the remnants of United's prewar squad with a number of the youngsters.

The war left its mark on United. German bombs had damaged Old Trafford in March 1941, an inevitability given its proximity to the docks and factories of Trafford Park. While repair work was carried out, United played home fixtures at Manchester City's Maine Road during their first season back.

By then, Gibson's vision was taking shape, with a core of local lads forming United's postwar team. In 1948, United won their first trophy of the Busby era, beating Stanley Matthews's Blackpool 4-2 in the FA Cup Final at Wembley. The majority of the players in the side had been raised within a few miles of Old Trafford, a clear sign that Gibson's grand plan to put faith in local youth was beginning to bear fruit. Gibson hadn't been able to attend the game due to ill health, but the team had taken the cup to his home as a gesture of gratitude on their return from Wembley.

When Gibson died in 1951, United's scouting network had already expanded beyond the Manchester area, overseen by chief scout Joe Armstrong. Edwards's arrival came as a result of this nationwide approach, as was the case with Bobby Charlton, who left his home in the north-east for Manchester the following year.

By the time United ended a 41-year wait to be English champions in 1952, they had already amassed the best crop of young players in English football and dominated the FA Youth Cup as a result. Younger players, including the likes of Gorton-born Roger Byrne, were already emerging in the first team. In the years to come, more would follow off the production line as Busby skilfully phased out some of the members of his first great United side and replaced them with talented, homegrown youngsters. Edwards, Dennis Viollet, Jackie Blanchflower, David Pegg and Eddie Colman were among a raft of youngsters to make inroads in the first team during this time; 21-year-old Tommy Taylor was also signed from Barnsley in 1953.

Incredibly, by the time Dad saw United play that afternoon against Huddersfield, the average age of the team had been just 21. The era of the 'Busby Babes' was dawning. The potential of the young side seemed boundless.

* * *

In 1944 David Harold Lloyd – my dad – was born in Victoria Park Maternity Home in Warrington, 12 miles or so from the then-bomb-damaged shell of Old Trafford. The early years of his life were spent in a cramped, smoke-stained terraced house on Owen Street, close to the centre of town. His parents had moved in in the same week they were married in 1933 and raised two daughters there, Margaret and Dorothy – Marg and Dot. They had hopes of one day moving the family out of the centre to somewhere more spacious, but the outbreak of war had put paid to their plans.

Warrington lies roughly in the very middle between Manchester and Liverpool. The River Mersey flows through its centre, the Manchester Ship Canal is just to the south. While the two cities either side of it were decimated by the Luftwaffe, Warrington, despite its industry and location, got off relatively lightly. The town remained relatively busy throughout the war years, thanks in part to the thousands of American servicemen stationed on the outskirts at RAF Burtonwood. For a time, the base became the largest US Army Air Force airfield outside the United States, continuing to be used by the Americans long after fighting in Europe had ended.

My grandad had been in his mid-30s when war began and was able to keep his job as a clerk instead of enlisting to fight. My grandmother, a small, dainty woman, had worked in the wire and textile factories close to their home, where her nimble fingers helped make her a skilled machinist. The family had next to nothing, and so, in the summer of 1943, the news that they were expecting a third child had come as a surprise.

Dad had few memories of Owen Street. He could vaguely recollect that the family had shared a toilet, which was in a separate brick outhouse in the backyard, and that his first kicks of a ball came in the cobbled street which ran along the back of the row. My grandparents continued to work as many hours as possible after the war, saving hard so that they could realise their ambition of running a pub together. By the time Dad turned five, they'd built up enough money and the family left Warrington for the Chat Moss pub in Glazebury, near the town of Leigh.

Growing up at the Chat Moss was one of the happiest times of Dad's life. The area surrounding it provided him with everything a boy of his age could have possibly wished for. To the rear was a bowling green he was sometimes allowed to play on and a small field fringed with several tall oak and lilac trees, which doubled up as natural climbing frames.

When the ground was dry enough, the field hosted small games of football between Dad and his school friends. It sloped gently away from the pub, down towards the banks of the River Glaze, which meandered through farmland before eventually joining the Mersey. In the summer, Dad would paddle or attempt to fish in the river. On one occasion, he'd told one of the pub's regulars, a man from Pennsylvania who was stationed at Burtonwood, of his ambitious plans to build a boat. The American returned the next afternoon with a US Army dingy deemed surplus to requirements at the base.

Nearly every day that summer, Dad and his friends carried the dingy over their heads along the road towards Leigh, cut across a farmer's field to the river bank, then set sail, floating a couple of miles downstream.

Dad had been granted plenty of freedom by his parents during that time. The running of the pub meant they were often busy but they trusted him to be sensible enough to keep out of bother. For most of the time he did, but, as is the way with most boys as they enter their teenage years, he and his mates had a tendency of being drawn to danger. The pub stood at the foot of a steep railway embankment, with the Manchester to Liverpool line running immediately along the side of it. The building was three storeys tall, with part of the top floor level with the tracks and so operating for a time as a ticket office for a small station. Most trains stopped at the station, but the occasional express train would thunder through at top speed, the pub's window panes rattling in their frames when it did.

In the far corner of the field at the back, out of sight of the pub, an old beech tree stood tall enough so that one of its branches hung directly above the tracks. Dad and his friends devised a game whereby they would take it in turns to dangle from the branch as an express train approached – a way of demonstrating their bravery. The game had come to an abrupt end one afternoon when they were caught by my grandmother, who was understandably furious at the thought of potentially having to explain how a child had been killed by a speeding train, right outside her pub. Dad took the brunt of it, but all involved in the game were required to help with the upkeep of the bowling green for several weeks as part of their apology.

The Chat Moss and its proximity to the railway, Dad always said, played an important part in his embryonic love of United. My grandfather's work had meant the Huddersfield game had been one of few occasions when they were able to see a match together when he was child. Crucially, though, that day showed Dad how accessible it was to him, even at such a young age. From that afternoon he attended fixtures with increasing regularity. Sometimes he'd go with eldest sister Marg, who had also been an avid United supporter, but more often with a small group of his school friends who were equally enamoured with Busby's young team.

By the early weeks of the 1955/56 season, Dad rarely missed a home game. He'd quickly realised that money was needed to pay for tickets and bus and train fares and had been proactive enough to get himself a job assisting a local milkman on his rounds in Leigh. Every Saturday that United were at home he would leave the pub early, often shortly after breakfast, arriving at the ground hours before kick-off.

Duncan was partly the reason for this. Barely a year on from first laying eyes on him gliding over the mud against Huddersfield, Dad's admiration for him had evolved into an obsession. Plenty of his spare time was spent scouring the sports pages of his dad's discarded newspapers for pictures of him to cut and paste to his bedroom wall.

For the entirety of Edwards's time with United, he lived in digs within walking distance of Old Trafford: first on Birch Avenue, close to the junction of Talbot Road and Warwick Road, then on Gorse Avenue, on the other side of Old Trafford cricket ground. He had quickly established himself as the jewel in the crown of Busby's young side, yet, despite his status, remained totally unassuming. While living at Gorse Avenue, he would accept invitations from local children to join in games of football in the street. On United's matchdays the same group of kids would follow him as he made his way to the stadium on foot. En route, Edwards would often wait for some of his team-mates at a bus stop close to a nearby pub, The Trafford. Dad and his friends came to know about this and would gather close by the bus stop before his arrival, just for the chance to spend a couple of minutes in his presence. In keeping with his modest nature, Edwards didn't seem to mind too much. The children were respectful and didn't hassle him for autographs and he seemed content to talk to those bold enough to ask him the odd question.

Dad never quite plucked up the courage to speak to his hero but vividly remembered the one occasion he walked beside him for a few yards on Warwick Road and Edwards briefly looked down at him and smiled. 'It felt like looking God in the eye,' he once described it.

Through the turnstiles, Dad and his mates often made for the same spot in the United Road stand, in line with the edge of the penalty area in front of the Stretford End. One of the advantages of being there so early was that they could claim one of the railings for themselves. On the days where the stand was crowded, getting an unobstructed view of the game was difficult for boys barely out of primary school. Perching on the railing solved this problem.

Dad watched United sweep to the First Division title in 1956. After a slender 2-1 defeat away to Preston North End in January, they had gone unbeaten for the remainder of the season, their strong finish another sign that an era of dominance lay before Busby's young side. The following campaign saw Bobby Charlton emerge from the youth ranks, scoring 12 times as United retained the title and reached the FA Cup Final, where they were denied the double by Aston Villa in controversial circumstances. After just six minutes, goalkeeper Ray Wood was left unconscious after being clattered by Villa forward Peter McParland. The collision was forceful enough to shatter Wood's cheekbone and he'd left the pitch as a result. Still in a time before the introduction of substitutes, United were forced to deploy Jackie Blanchflower as a makeshift goalkeeper and lost 2-1 – McParland scoring both Villa goals.

More importantly, 1956/57 was also the season when United became the first English club to enter into European competition. Chelsea, England's champions in 1955, had been invited to take part in the inaugural European Cup a year earlier but had been pressured into rejecting the offer by organisers of the Football League, who believed the new competition to be a distraction. Twelve months on, United ignored similar calls and signed up.

The thought of seeing a group of players he saw every other Saturday flying off to far corners of the continent captured Dad's imagination. United's first European tie was played in Brussels, where they beat Anderlecht 2-0 in the first leg of a preliminary round. A fortnight later, Dad had his first taste of Maine Road, which United used for the return leg due to a lack of floodlights at Old Trafford. United won 10-0, seeing them through to a first-round tie with Borussia Dortmund.

Their first European adventure finally came to an end in the semi-final against reigning champions Real Madrid. Playing before a crowd of over 130,000 in the first leg in Spain, Busby's side held out for an hour before Real took the lead, then doubled it almost instantly through the legendary Alfredo Di Stéfano. Taylor halved the deficit late on but United immediately conceded a third, dashing hopes that they might reach the final. Real killed the tie in the first half of the return leg under Old Trafford's newly installed floodlights; Raymond Kopa and Héctor Rial put them 5-1 up on aggregate. Though goals from Taylor and Charlton saw United fight back to level at 2-2 on the night, Real deservedly progressed, going on to beat Fiorentina and retain their title.

Naturally, there was disappointment that United had come up short against Madrid, but solace could be gleaned from the fact that the team was still incredibly young. Real had the edge at that moment, but Busby had built an exciting side made up of honest, working-class lads – sons of Salford and Barnsley and Dudley, who, despite their age, had already proven they could go up against the likes of Di Stéfano, Gento and Kopa and compete.

As they matured, they would improve. Surpassing Real and conquering Europe would be well within their grasp with time on their side. All Busby had to do was keep the group together and continental success would surely come. Perhaps, had fate not intervened in such an unfathomably cruel way, it may have arrived the very next year.

On 6 February 1958, Dad finished the school day at Leigh Boys' Grammar and went into the town centre to run some errands for my grandmother. By the time he returned to the pub, it was early evening and darkness was falling. His parents had been sitting at the table in the room at the back of the bar area, waiting. At first, they hadn't said a thing, as if expecting him to greet them with more than just hello. When he didn't, my grandad had spoken, 'Have you heard the news, son?'

Dad hadn't, and shook his head, baffled.

Chapter 3

Bryan Robson wouldn't cry

AFTER THE Bournemouth game, Dad didn't go back to Old Trafford for nearly two months. On Boxing Day I woke to a text from my mum explaining that he'd been up all night feeling unwell and wouldn't be up to going with me to see United play Burnley later that day.

It was probably no bad thing, I thought on the drive home that evening; United were awful and fortunate to scrape a 2-2 draw.

Four days later, he was still feeling rough and missed a somehow even more tedious draw with Southampton. By then it was clear he had been struck down with a bout of flu, which lingered on into the new year, the tail-end of it causing him to miss an FA Cup tie with Derby as well. For him to miss two games in succession was a rarity, but *three* – even when factoring how densely packed the fixture list is around that time of year – was unheard of.

He remained bed-bound for the best part of a fortnight, his phone left uncharged in a drawer downstairs. My mum gave updates, assuring me it was 'just a bug', nothing more. She admitted that he could have probably made the Derby game but didn't want to risk setting himself back a week by sitting out in the cold for a couple of hours. He would be fine, I was told regularly – almost *too* regularly.

In the middle of January, United played Stoke in the league on a Wednesday night. Dad had recovered by then and, as far as I knew, planned on making his Old Trafford return. I was down to cover the game with work, so dropped my season ticket off at his house earlier that week in the hope that Chris would take him.

The press box at Old Trafford was directly opposite our block on the other side of the pitch. From there, I could just about pick out our seats under the shadow cast by the roof of the Sir Alex Ferguson Stand. Whenever I'd been at a game in a media capacity in the past, I'd glance up at kick-off and see Dad frantically waving down at me with both arms, just to be absolutely certain I knew he was there. But as the Stoke game started, I only saw two empty seats. I'd hoped he was simply running slightly late, that the traffic had snarled up somewhere along the way. Twenty minutes into the first half, though, I glanced up again during a break in play and there was still no sign of him. I accepted he wasn't coming. *Four games in a row.*

I'd started to wonder, the longer he stayed away, if he'd return to Old Trafford at all. Perhaps it wasn't 'just a bug', and the cancer had actually taken hold somewhere else in the time since his last scan. Maybe that explained the other stuff, too. When someone you care about has lived with cancer for a while, you're prone to such paranoia. It crossed my mind that, perhaps without realising it, that miserable, rain-lashed Wednesday night against Bournemouth had been our last game together. I hated that thought – that the final memory I would have of watching a match with him might be that distant look on his face after he'd asked me for a second time where Wayne Rooney was.

The day after Bournemouth I'd been working in Manchester. My mum had been in the city centre to do some Christmas shopping, so I met in her a quiet corner of the coffee shop in Waterstones on Deansgate. I told her about what had happened the previous night and my wider concerns about Dad's change in behaviour since the start of the season. She nodded along wordlessly as I spoke, then, when I'd finished, told me she'd been relieved to hear it. Everything I'd said – the long spells of silence, the moments of inexplicable confusion – tied in with what she had experienced at home over the course of several months. She hadn't wanted to burden me or Chris with it until either of us had said something to her. Now presented with the opportunity, the dam burst.

My mum couldn't be sure when it had begun, but the first thing she noticed was how Dad had started to keep himself to himself around the house, as if deliberately avoiding contact. He would take himself out to the garage to do an unspecified and not very urgent job, or, more commonly, say he was tired and sit himself in his chair in front of the TV and doze off to sleep for a whole afternoon. He no longer bothered reading the paper in a morning. The daily crossword and sudoku puzzles he would once have boxed off before midday were left untouched.

As time passed, she had noticed other things. His handwriting changed. Names became a problem. He'd started referring to Maisie, their dog of nearly eight years, as Sally, the brilliant, permanently overweight black Labrador we'd had as the family dog when Chris and I were kids. After initially correcting him a few times, it happened so frequently she forced herself to ignore it.

The week before Bournemouth, she very nearly called me. Early one afternoon, she had asked Dad if he would mind nipping down the road to the local shop for a loaf of bread. It would only take ten minutes there and back, even at his pace. Nearly an hour later, when he hadn't come back, she'd started to worry. As she'd been about to dial my number, however, the front door had finally opened. There he was, minus the loaf of bread. Bewilderingly, he handed over a box of four cakes, then sat himself down in his usual spot in the chair in front of the TV. That was the moment she knew something was seriously awry, her own 'Where's Rooney?' moment.

We finished our coffee and agreed to keep a close eye on him over Christmas. Beyond the cancer, we didn't speculate what the cause might be. I promised to be even more vigilant at the football, unaware it would take so long before we attended another game together.

* * *

United edged their way through January. Draws around Christmas saw them lose even more ground on City, who added to the nauseatingly wide lead they'd already opened up after the derby win in December. Three league wins in a row – one of which being the Stoke game – briefly lifted spirits, as did the arrival of Alexis Sánchez from Arsenal, but a humbling by Tottenham at Wembley at the end of the month burned away the optimism that had been building.

Three days after the Spurs game, Dad finally went back. United welcomed Huddersfield to Old Trafford in their first match of February. He had made it known through my mum, who was still in the mediator role she had first assumed while he had been laid up with the flu, that he wanted to come.

The 60th anniversary of Munich fell in the middle of the following week. Arrangements had been made for a special service to take place inside Old Trafford on the day itself, but a smaller ceremony was being held at the foot of the memorial plaque at the side of the East Stand before kick-off.

Dad hadn't been up to the walk over from the usual car park so Chris offered to drop us as close to the ground as the matchday traffic allowed and promised to pick us up somewhere close by after full time. Out of the car, we slowly made our way through the throngs to where a small platform had been erected beneath the memorial. Scarves and flowers had been laid on the floor around it, the ink on the handwritten messages attached to them beginning to blur and run in the light drizzle. Prayers were read, songs were sung. There was a moment of quiet reflection to remember the lives lost, then the service ended and the crowds drifted away towards the turnstiles. Dad hung on for a moment or two longer, saying nothing, looking up at the names etched into the plaque. With a slight shake of his head, he eventually traipsed away.

It's difficult for an outsider to fully grasp how much of a shadow Munich still casts over United. It was, after all, something which happened a long time ago. Most who go the games now weren't alive then and could never truly appreciate how devastating the days and weeks that followed the crash were, and the toll it took on the club and the city. That's what makes the events which mark the anniversaries so important. The numbers of those of an age to remember February 1958 dwindle with every passing year, but it's on these occasions you see how much it means to that older generation of supporter, how raw it remains despite decades passing and nearly entire lives being lived. For the rest of us, it's on those days you get the closest sense of how bleak that period of time was. Dad was one of several supporters who attended games before Munich in our block. Frank had been a regular. There was also Sue, a lady from Saddleworth who sat on the other side of Nige and religiously brought a bag of hard-boiled sweets to hand out to us all at half-time. She, I think, had also started going around that time. Years earlier I'd noticed that while they regularly shared memories of Duncan and the Babes and the days *before* Munich, never once did they ever discuss *Munich*. That, I thought, was telling.

We got to our seats in time to see a large surfer banner unfurled and passed along the lower tier of the Stretford End.

'WE'LL NEVER DIE' read the large black and red lettering which ran across it, beneath an image of 11 young men lining up beside each other on a football pitch in Belgrade, unaware they were about to play their final game together.

With the banner in position, the players were summoned to the centre circle for a minute's silence. As it neared its end, I heard Dad make a couple of sniffling noises in quick succession and realised he was crying. I didn't turn to look at him until the minute's silence had ended. As I did, he lifted his arm to his face, attempting to wipe away any trace of tears from his cheeks with the sleeve of his coat.

'You all right?' I asked, feeling awkwardly compelled to force something out.

'Fine,' he replied, just as I expected him to, and the game kicked off.

Dad had never been one for showing he was upset. Not long after he'd first started dating my mum, he told her how he'd been brought up that way: to get on with things, to not make a fuss. Showing emotion wasn't something he was comfortable with – a sign of weakness, even. For this reason, I never once saw him cry when I was a child. Even when his parents died, at a time when he clearly *must* have been upset, he came downstairs the next morning and took himself off to work, as though all was normal.

It was something he tried to instil into my brother and me from an early age. On a caravan holiday somewhere in the south of France one summer I fell off a swing and badly grazed my knee as I landed. I'd screamed the campsite down at the first sight of blood and kept going until well after he'd dug out the first-aid kit from the boot of his car. He'd quickly grown impatient with me and ordered me to stop the crying. 'Bryan Robson wouldn't cry over a thing like this,' he'd snapped, which, looking back, is hilarious. I was four. I didn't have a clue who Bryan Robson was.

It was the cancer – or rather, the cancer treatment – that changed him. He was first diagnosed in the autumn of 2006. I'd been living away at university in Leeds when he'd called me one October afternoon to say he'd something to tell me, but insisted he wanted to do it in person. He had initially considered driving over to my student halls that same night, but United were at home to Benfica in the Champions League so he suggested I met him at Old Trafford instead. He would sort me a ticket out and would pay my train fare home. I met him outside the East Stand, where he immediately told me the news: he had prostate cancer which required urgent treatment. He kept it brief and very matter-of-fact, insisting he'd be fine and wasn't about to die, then we walked over to Sam Platt's pub for a pre-match pint and talked about the starting XI.

I don't remember all the details leading to his diagnosis now, but he'd become aware that he'd needed to go to the toilet a lot – so much so that it had started to mean he couldn't leave the house without pre-planning stops to avoid accidents. Typically, he'd buried his head in the sand about how serious it might have been and became adept at hiding it from my mum. On a holiday in Italy that summer it reached a point where it was impossible to keep it a secret.

The good news, the oncologist had told him, was that the cancer hadn't broken free of the prostate. That meant he was eligible to undergo a form of treatment known as 'permanent seed brachytherapy', which involved radioactive seeds the size of rice grains being implanted in his prostate. The seeds would blast the cancer cells with a constant stream of radiation for several weeks, then become redundant.

Alongside this, Dad also underwent hormone treatment to reduce the amount of testosterone his body produced. Prostate cancer cells usually need testosterone to grow. By limiting or in some cases blocking it altogether, the cells will usually shrink. There are plenty of potential side effects to the hormone treatment. Many men experience changes to their mood: they can become angry, or find themselves crying a lot. The latter was the case with Dad, which, given his lifelong attitude towards openly showing emotion, he found extremely embarrassing. Initially, as he adjusted to the treatment, he found himself spontaneously bursting into tears at the slightest of things. Once, memorably, the sight of a baby smiling at him while he waited in the checkout queue in Tesco had been enough to set him off.

Gradually, the outbursts eased to the point where he found he could control them. Football, though, still had a tendency to draw them to the surface every once in a while.

In 2016, we'd gone down to Wembley for the FA Cup semi-final against Everton. Our tickets had us close to the end of our row, high up in the nosebleed section near to one of the big screens. The two seats between us and the steps leading towards the exit had remained empty until about 15 minutes after kick-off, when two lads – both half-cut and speaking in slurred Salford accents – came stumbling up towards us. One of them marked his arrival by crouching down and snorting some cocaine straight off his seat as a nearby steward pretended not to notice. Dad, naturally, felt uncomfortable.

The game was tense. United scored first through Maurouane Fellaini but Everton created and squandered numerous decent chances before half-time. After missing a penalty in the second half they drew level minutes later when Chris Smalling sliced a cross into his own goal. It was nervy from then on, remaining on a knife-edge until stoppage time when, with extra time looming, an off-balance Ander Herrera managed to stab a pass through a tiny gap into the path of Anthony Martial, who suddenly found himself clean through on the goal down below us. Martial kept his head and slotted the ball into the corner, sparking bedlam in the

United end. I tumbled three or four rows forward, cutting my shin as I went and thudding the side of my head against the edge of someone's seat. I picked myself up, dazed but still celebrating, then wondered if Dad had also been swept from his position in the avalanche that followed the goal. He hadn't. He remained standing in the same spot, bawling his eyes out. The two coke-fuelled lads from Salford had cut short their own celebrations to tend to him, one of them tenderly holding Dad's head against his chest as he sobbed. He saw me, held up a clenched fist and shook it in celebration, then continued sobbing.

* * *

The banner on the Stretford End disappeared after the minute's silence had come to an end. From kick-off, Huddersfield sat deep, content to try and frustrate. For the first 45 minutes their plan worked: United dominated the ball but looked ponderous when it arrived in the final third of the pitch. Romelu Lukaku, whose steady stream of early season goals had slowed, was hardly involved. Sánchez, making his home debut, looked rusty and out of tune with his new team-mates.

In isolation, 45 goalless minutes against a team set up to dig in and play for a point could be ignored, but this kind of toothless display had become a regular thing. Nige complained loudly from his seat in front of us as the half drew to a close. His concerns about José Mourinho and the direction in which the team appeared to be drifting had grown substantially since the turn of the year. To the amusement of those of us who sat behind him, his outbursts were becoming more frequent and taking place earlier and earlier with every passing game.

I was encouraged that Dad, having composed himself after the minute's silence, seemed to be showing an interest in the game during the early minutes. It didn't amount to more than the odd short sentence, but it was enough to show he was at least following what was going on. Alas, his observations quickly dried up and he sat silently with his arms folded until the fourth official lifted the board to show stoppage time – his cue to head for the toilets.

I had come to accept during his four-match absence that this was no temporary thing. The days of Dad excitedly grabbing me in the aftermath of an important goal had gone; I would never watch him hold his own in one of the more animated pre-game concourse debates about team selections or which players needed selling. It was a miserable thought, but I consoled myself with the fact that he was at least back; our time going to the football together wasn't quite done. Fergie Time, perhaps, but not *full* time.

In the second half, United found a breakthrough. Having looked noticeably sharper than they had in the first 45, the ball was fed to Juan Mata, who clipped a cross from the left wing towards the near post, where Lukaku had stolen a yard from his marker and steered a volleyed finish beyond the goalkeeper. A second came soon after. Paul Pogba had reportedly fallen out with Mourinho in the build-up to the game, and was only named on the bench. On as a substitute, he floated a diagonal pass over the top of the Huddersfield defence for Mata, who plucked the ball from the sky with an immaculate first touch, pirouetted way from a defender, then laid it across the edge of the area to Sánchez, who was tripped just inside. Sánchez's penalty was saved but the ball fell back at his feet, allowing him to tuck away the rebound. Game over. With plenty of time to spare the crowd settled, the frustration of the first half forgotten.

Not long after the Sánchez goal, Dad mumbled something about leaving before the end of the game. This had come as a surprise; he staunchly believed that football supporters were duty-bound to stay until the end, regardless of how good or bad the result was likely to be. If beating the traffic mattered more to you, you were doing it wrong, he'd say. In 1999, during the home leg of the semi-final against Juventus, I'd seen him berate a guy for getting up and leaving ten minutes before the end, with United a goal down. The bloke had ignored him on his way out. After the celebrations for Ryan Giggs's equaliser in stoppage time had begun to calm down, he'd jabbed his finger into my shoulder. 'That's why you stay to the end,' he'd yelled.

After I'd ignored his initial request, he'd reiterated his wish to leave minutes later. Mindful of the promise I'd made my mum the day after the Bournemouth game, I reluctantly agreed. Avoiding the rush after the full-time whistle seemed a wise decision, especially given my brother would be waiting for us somewhere nearby. With a head start on everyone else, we'd be home inside half an hour.

The plan quickly fell apart. Out of the lift at the bottom of Sir Alex Ferguson Stand, we skirted the outside of the stadium towards the East Stand, waiting for my phone to catch a signal. When it did, I phoned Chris, who told me he was running late – so late, in fact, that we had to sit ourselves down on a bench close to the Holy Trinity statue and watch the crowds we'd expected to beat gush out of the exits after full time. When the initial surge had slowed to a trickle, Chris called to say he was still stuck in traffic at the top of Trafford Road. I relayed the message to Dad, who wearily hauled himself to his feet with an exasperated huff. I continued the call, giving a brief summary of the game. I didn't stay on long but it dawned on me just as I was about to end the call that Dad was no longer standing next to me. I'd briefly panicked, before spotting the back of his coat in the distance. He'd returned to the memorial.

I hung back for a couple of minutes, allowing him some privacy while keeping an eye on him to be sure he didn't wander off elsewhere. When the moment felt apt to eventually join him, his eyes were brimming with tears again. Fixed to the brickwork beneath the plaque was a smaller, framed version of the image which had covered the large surfer banner we'd seen inside the ground earlier – that of the United team in Belgrade, the pitch behind them flecked with clumps of snow.

'Who's who?' I asked, then felt an immediate sting of guilt at how insensitive the question was. This was a man who struggled to correctly name his own dog, for fuck's sake. Asking him to recite the names of 11 men whose names he'd known in childhood was bordering on cruel.

But then, narrowing his eyes slightly as he focused on the faces on the picture, he began to speak.

'Duncan, Coleman, Jones,' he uttered, voice cracking. 'Morgans, Charlton, Viollet, Taylor and Foulkes.' A pause. 'The goalkeeper's Harry Gregg. Then it's Scanlon. And that's Roger Byrne on the end.'

Another pause.

'God, you should have seen them play.'

Chapter 4

Munich

ON THE morning of 7 February 1958, Dad awoke to find his mother perched on the edge of his bed watching over him, brow furrowed with concern. He'd pulled himself up from beneath the sheets to sit beside her, then, in his bleary-eyed state, began recounting the terribly vivid dream he'd had overnight. There had been a plane crash, he told her. United had been on the plane. Some of the players had been killed.

She had reached out before he could say any more, grabbing one of his hands and gently clasping it between hers.

'It's true, love,' she'd said, softly. 'It wasn't a dream.'

For a matter of seconds, he'd wondered if he was still trapped inside the nightmare and willed himself to wake up. When he didn't, the sickening realisation washed over him. He remembered the moment his father had broken the news of the crash to him when he'd returned home the previous night; how they'd sat together until gone midnight taking in the intermittent news reports on the TV and radio. The first grainy black-and-white footage he'd seen of the stricken aircraft – the twisted metal and debris strewn across the snow – had hit hard, as had the moment the newsreader confirmed that some of the team he adored were dead.

He hadn't cried. That would come later. After details of just how serious the crash was had started to emerge, a strange numbness had set in – a sense that what had taken place in Munich that Thursday somehow wasn't quite real. Dad was almost certainly dealing with some form of shock, perhaps explaining why his brain had convinced him it had been a dream when he'd first stirred from sleep the next morning. The possibility that it *might* have been true was simply too traumatic, too horrific for him to accept.

Having snatched barely a couple of hours of fitful sleep through the night, Dad nearly didn't go to school that day. Naively believing it to be the best thing to take his mind off events, his mother had insisted he went and, to make sure he did, walked with him to the bus stop shortly after breakfast.

Some of the gang of boys who went to the games with him had caught the same school bus. The short Friday-morning journey into Leigh was often a time for fine-tuning arrangements for going to Old Trafford the following day. On this occasion, though, there had been no such talk, only a swirl of rumours flying back and forth about which players had and hadn't survived. It barely felt real.

When he reached school, the atmosphere had been sombre, no more so than later in the morning, when an assembly had been called in the hall. The silence before it began was interrupted by a younger boy, who'd started to cry. Hearing this was enough. Dad, along with several other boys, also began to weep. The assembly had almost been cancelled.

United had secured their place in the semi-finals of the European Cup for a second year running that Wednesday. Having beaten Red Star Belgrade 2-1 at Old Trafford in January, they roared into a commanding 3-0 lead in little over half an hour in Yugoslavia. Dennis Viollet scored inside two minutes before Bobby Charlton added a couple more. Up 5-1 on aggregate, they were cruising. In the second half, though, Red Star battled back, scoring three quick-fire goals before the game had reached the hour mark. Despite a nervy climax, United held out.

That night, the team attended a banquet hosted by Red Star at a hotel in central Belgrade. They were due back in Manchester the next afternoon ahead of a crucial encounter with league leaders Wolverhampton Wanderers, scheduled for the Saturday afternoon. Returning from a midweek match on the far side of the continent presented obvious problems, but Busby, irritated by the Football League's stuffy attitude towards United competing in Europe, was determined his side made it back for the game.

Busby ordered his team to rise early for the return journey. With some of his players nursing sore heads from the night before, they made their way to the airport and through customs. The Airspeed AS.57 Ambassador aircraft carrying United wasn't capable of flying non-stop from Belgrade to Manchester, so, as it had done on the outbound trip, it broke the journey by stopping to refuel in Munich.

After midday, the plane reached Munich-Riem Airport, where thick snow blanketed much of the surrounding area. All onboard were directed to the warmth of the terminal building while the aircraft was prepared for the final leg of the journey. Soon after, they were called back to the plane, which promptly set off down the runway, gradually picking up speed. Then, foreshadowing the tragedy to come, the plane had shuddered and came to an abrupt halt. In the cockpit, captain James Thain blamed a fluctuation of boost pressure for the aborted take-off, but calmly instructed those onboard to keep their seatbelts fastened as they taxied back towards the start of the runway for a second attempt. Minutes later, the plane came to a sharp stop once again, Thain citing further concerns over boost surging.

All passengers briefly returned to the terminal building. By then, it appeared the second leg of the journey would be postponed until the next day. Edwards had even sent a telegram to his landlady at Gorse Avenue explaining as much. But after 15 minutes the passengers were summoned back to the plane. Thain believed the surging problem could be overcome by opening the throttle more slowly, which would be helped by Munich-Riem's lengthy runway.

The atmosphere onboard had been tense, so much so that, before the third take-off attempt, several passengers opted to move towards the back of the aircraft in the belief it was safer.

Again, the plane picked up speed. Again, the surging problem recurred, prompting co-pilot Kenneth Rayment to ease off on the throttle before pushing forwards again. Seconds later, Thain announced that the plane had reached V1: the speed at which a take-off attempt could not be aborted. The next important milestone would be V2, when the plane was travelling fast enough to lift into the air. To the horror of Thain and Rayment, however, the needle on the air-speed indicator began to drop sharply. With the end of the runway in sight the plane was yet to reach V2, but travelling too fast to stop.

The passengers first became aware that something was drastically wrong when the plane smashed through a perimeter fence at the end of the runway, sending a forceful jolt through the aircraft. Shortly after, one of its wings was torn off as it collided with a house, setting the building alight. The tail broke away. A huge hole was ripped open in the side of the fuselage. The plane ploughed on, disintegrating as it went. The cockpit slammed into a copse of trees, while another part of the plane careered into a wooden hut, which had housed a truck loaded with fuel. The impact caused a huge explosion. Then, for a few seconds before the wail of sirens could be heard, there was an eerie silence.

Twenty people died at the scene. Among them were seven of United's brilliant young team: Geoff Bent, Roger Byrne,

Eddie Colman, Mark Jones, David Pegg, Tommy Taylor and Billy Whelan. Club secretary Walter Crickmer was also killed, as were Tom Curry and Bert Whalley – two of Busby's coaching staff – and several journalists who had travelled with the team to cover the game in Belgrade.

Countless more were injured, some seriously. Frank Swift, the former Manchester City goalkeeper turned journalist, became the 21st victim when he died in an ambulance. There were major concerns about Busby, too, along with some of the surviving players – namely Johnny Berry and the great Duncan Edwards.

Back in Manchester, huge crowds formed around newsstands on the evening of the crash as word began to filter through. There were similar scenes the following day. Many local fans gathered at Old Trafford, waiting for word from the club. As the facts became known, the desperate clamour for information steadily subsided, replaced by a deep sense of mourning which gripped the entire city and beyond. On the Saturday afternoon, when United should have hosted Wolves in a potential league title decider, many supporters flocked to the ground in their droves once again, seeking comfort from the crowd.

Dad, distraught, couldn't face it and opted not to leave the confines of his own bedroom that weekend. His mother and sisters took it in turns to check in on him, leaving his meals on the landing floor by his door.

Within a week of the crash, the coffins of those who had perished were flown back to Manchester where they were to be held in Old Trafford's old gymnasium until the respective funerals took place. Hearing about their arrival, Dad had suddenly felt a need to be there. Without giving it a second thought, he'd slipped on to an afternoon train to Eccles and, in the absence of the usual matchday buses queuing at the station front, he set out to complete the rest of his journey to the stadium on foot. He didn't quite make it that far. As he approached, the crowds lining the roadside thickened until there was no space on the pavements. With darkness falling, he took up a position on the kerb about half a mile away and watched the procession of black cars carrying the coffins slowly pass by. Some of the bystanders bowed their heads as they did; others wept. A woman standing close by had been so overcome by emotion that she collapsed to her knees and had to be helped back up.

Dad hadn't returned home until late. So consumed by his need to be there, he hadn't thought to tell anyone back at the pub where he was. His parents, already concerned by their son's behaviour and general state of mind since the crash, had grown increasingly worried as the evening drew on. This immediately switched to anger when he walked through the door.

Amid the grief, difficult discussions were held about United's return to action. Games had been postponed in the aftermath of the tragedy, but in time the fixture list needed to be honoured. It was clear that when United did play their next match, Busby wouldn't be there to see it. After suffering multiple injuries, his chances of survival had hung in the balance for several days – to the extent that he was twice read the last rites. After overcoming the worst of it, it was apparent he would require a lengthy spell in hospital as he recovered.

The responsibility of taking charge of the team fell to Busby's long-term assistant, Jimmy Murphy, who he'd recruited after a chance meeting in Italy in the spring of 1945. Busby, having recently agreed to take the United job by then, had been manager of the British Army football team towards the end of World War II and was completing the last of his military duties in Bari when he observed Murphy, a former West Bromwich Albion wing-half, taking a session for

NCOs. Impressed by what he saw, he offered him a position on his staff.

Murphy played a significant role in shaping the club's successes. He was responsible for training the young players, ensuring they were ready for their transition to the first team when the time came. Having first met them as teenagers, Murphy nurtured the talents of nearly all of the 1958 side and was particularly close to them as a result. A proud Welshman, Murphy's ability as a coach had seen him take charge of his national side in 1956, a position he held alongside his role at United. His responsibilities with Wales saw him miss the game in Belgrade to oversee a World Cup qualifier with Israel in Cardiff. He'd returned to Manchester on the evening of the crash completely unaware of events in Munich. The responsibility of breaking the awful news to him fell to a teary-eyed club secretary. He'd grabbed a bottle of whiskey and locked himself away in a nearby office, crying for several hours.

Murphy visited Busby as he recuperated in Munich and was instructed him to keep things in order until he was back. On his return to England, Murphy swiftly set about putting together a squad that would allow United to finish the season. That, cruelly, had become the only objective from a football perspective. Talk of European Cups and a league title decider against Wolves had been rendered irrelevant.

A barely recognisable United team returned to action just two weeks to the day of their game in Belgrade. Back at Old Trafford, 60,000 people flooded through the turnstiles for the FA Cup fifth round tie against Sheffield Wednesday. Remarkably, two Munich survivors started the game: Bill Foulkes, named as captain, and Harry Gregg, who after the crash had bravely risked his own life by pulling several survivors clear of the burning wreckage. Carried by an emotionally charged crowd, United's threadbare side somehow ran out

3-0 victors. Foulkes, having maintained focus throughout the 90 minutes, broke down when the full-time whistle sounded.

Dad, despite his best efforts, didn't attend the Sheffield Wednesday match. His parents' fury at the nature of his visit to Old Trafford the previous week had not dimmed and they made it explicitly clear that he would not, under any circumstances, be allowed to go. As the game drew nearer he had hoped their stance might have softened, but a couple of tentative attempts to persuade them to reconsider proved futile. Begrudgingly, he accepted their decision.

His parents were incredibly supportive with him during that period. Along with his two older sisters, they recognised the depth of his devotion to his team and how much of a toll such a traumatic event would have taken. He found out years later that his mother, who had absolutely doted on him, had barely slept for weeks after Munich, pacing the pub in the small hours of the morning, worrying about him. His father would sit with him through every news report and had insisted on the pair of them taking an evening walk nearly every night to allow him time to talk and clear his head. Though they had to put their foot down over the Sheffield Wednesday game, they had also compromised in agreeing for him to go to the league match with Nottingham Forest the following Saturday. They realised how important it was for him to go back as soon as he could.

Through his heartbreak, Dad clung to hope that Duncan might pull through. That, though a small mercy given the other lives that had been lost, became something to focus upon.

Edwards had been one of the passengers who moved towards the back of the aircraft ahead of the doomed third take-off attempt. His broken body had been pulled from the wreckage at the crash site and taken to Rechts der Isar Hospital, where most of the injured were treated in the aftermath. Doctors and nurses had worked tirelessly to keep him alive. He'd suffered a collapsed lung, several broken ribs, a broken pelvis and multiple fractures to his right femur. Even if he survived, there was a distinct possibility that he might never walk again, let alone return to playing football. It was the damage to his kidneys, however, which posed the most serious threat to his life. The doctors had been amazed when he was admitted. Most people with similar injuries would have been expected to die at the scene or in the ambulance. The odds were still piled high against him, but the strength he'd shown just to reach the hospital had been enough to raise the faintest glimmer of hope that he might, somehow, survive.

Updates on Edwards's condition were released twice daily by the hospital, relayed over the radio to those waiting for word in England. Dad would rush home from school each day, where my grandfather would greet him at the door with the latest.

Nearly a week after the crash, Edwards began to stir from his coma. When his eyes opened, he'd been confused by his surroundings and unaware of the full extent of what had happened. Those caring for him were under strict instruction not to divulge much in the way of information about the crash to the seriously injured. He quickly became agitated and was particularly upset that he'd lost a watch gifted to him after the semi-final against Real Madrid the previous year. Fortunately, the watch had been discovered among the wreckage of the plane and was quickly fastened to his wrist, helping him settle.

Edwards had briefly spoken to Murphy while he visited the hospital, asking him what time the title decider against Wolves would kick off. The game had of course been postponed, but Murphy played along so as not to give any clues as to the crushing truth of what had taken place. Bobby Charlton, one of Edwards's closest friends on the team, had also spent several days in the hospital following the crash. After learning he was to be discharged, he paid Edwards a visit. 'I've been waiting for you,' Edwards, in obvious pain, had said to his friend. 'Where the bloody hell have you been?' It was the last time the pair would speak. On the afternoon of 11 February, the nitrogen levels in Edwards's blood spiked. With his condition deteriorating, his parents dashed from their home in Dudley to catch a flight from London to Munich to be at his bedside. An artificial kidney was rushed to the hospital the next day and Edwards was hooked up to the machine as soon as it arrived. He had been in a coma again and close to death the following morning, but the machine seemed to be working. The next day he woke and asked where he was before being allowed a drink of milk. The following days saw his condition rise and fall several times, the medical staff astounded by his strength. By the 17th, there was even quiet optimism among those treating him that his damaged kidneys were showing signs that they were starting to work. Again, though, just as there had been a hint of hope, things took another turn for the worse.

By the 19th, he was weak following further treatment from the artificial kidney machine and having undergone person-to-person blood transfusions. Doctors were again pessimistic about his chances of survival. In the early hours of the 21st, having entered a deep sleep, Duncan passed away. He was 21 years of age.

Word reached the pub later that day, where Dad had been distraught. For a fortnight he'd struggled to come to terms with the initial horrors of the crash, but, for reasons he could never fully articulate, Duncan's death seemed to amplify the already deep sense of loss. The timing no doubt played a part – that he died a couple of weeks after the others had reopened barely healed wounds – but the simple fact it was *him* who suffered such a painful, drawn-out end was likely also a factor. Nobody represented the spirit of Busby's brilliant young team quite like Duncan. He was a colossus, the great hope of English football and a future captain for club and country. Even at the dawn of his career, he was already on the cusp of greatness. It was inconceivable that he could be gone, cut down in his prime.

The following day was the Saturday of the league game with Forest. Dad had only two memories of it. The first was that he, for the first time in a long time, decided against getting the early train. There would be no need to crowd around the bus stop on Warwick Road and wait for Duncan now. Those days were gone. The second was after he'd got inside Old Trafford and took up a position in the usual place, next to the railing. Before kick-off, he and a friend had leaned against it, talking, when they'd suddenly become aware of how crowded the terrace behind them had become. Very quickly, the sheer volume of grieving supporters entering the ground had pushed them forward, the weight pinning their chests against the railing. Fortunately, two of the men immediately behind had recognised they were struggling and, on the count of three, pushed back against the crowd to allow them just enough space to duck beneath the rail and avoid being crushed.

The game had ended 1-1. Forest had scored first before Alex Dawson had equalised 15 minutes from time. The draw meant United lost more ground on Wolves in a title race which, of course, no longer mattered.

For those in the crowd, attending a football match had never been less about the football itself.

Chapter 5

The last games

HAVING MUSTERED just enough energy to go to the Huddersfield match in early February, Dad attended just four more games before his last: Chelsea, Liverpool and Arsenal in the league – all wins – and the unmitigated disaster of a showing against Sevilla in the Champions League last 16, which had proved to be his final European game.

It was a night in which Nige's simmering frustration towards José Mourinho's management had, in the last 15 minutes, erupted into a volley of unabated, foul-mouthed fury – reaching a point where, concerned he might be turfed out by a steward or scream himself into bursting an important blood vessel in his head, a couple of those around him had leaned over for a quiet word.

United had escaped the first leg with a goalless draw in Spain, thanks largely to a scarcely believable point-blank save from David de Gea. Despite their hit-and-miss form, the home leg was deemed winnable, especially with a big European night atmosphere behind them.

It didn't work out that way. United seemed to start brightly, zipping the ball about with purpose but without really creating much in the way of openings. Gradually, as time went on, Sevilla settled and had a couple of half-decent chances of their own. As they did, United's confidence began to drain away and the game became more cagey and low-risk. Goalless at half-time, there was a strong feeling that whoever scored first would progress to the quarters. Sure enough, that proved to be the case.

Approaching the last 15 minutes, Wissam Ben Yedder came on as a substitute and, with almost his first touch, slotted a low shot beyond De Gea for the first goal of the game. This triggered Nige's expletive-laden tirade. Ben Yedder exploited shoddy marking at a corner to score a second minutes later. Stunned into urgency, United pulled one back through Romelu Lukaku but squandered numerous more opportunities as full time approached. They were out.

Watching Nige furiously storm out at the end, it struck me that results like this – the really bad ones – didn't seem to hurt in the same way they once had. Years ago, European exits had really stung, enough to ruin entire weeks. Porto in 2004 had been just about the worst of the lot, particularly after Paul Scholes had seen a perfectly legitimate goal ruled out for offside before the Portuguese – then managed by Mourinho, of course – had landed the killer blow through Costinha's late away goal. Perhaps, I thought, it was me being that bit older and more mature, or that my expectations of my team simply weren't as high as they once were after their continuing failed attempts to pull themselves out of the post-Ferguson nuclear winter.

In hindsight, I see now that it was more likely my growing concern about Dad that was suppressing my feelings towards United and football in general. He had, after all, been a near-constant when it came to me watching football, by my side for nearly every game I'd ever taken in. Though he still attended sporadically, each matchday brought reminders that all was not well.

Earlier that same night, for example, before Sevilla had scored their first goal, Dad hadn't returned to his seat after half-time. After what felt like an eternity but was probably no more than five minutes I'd been worried enough to leave my own seat and head down below to look for him. When he wasn't in the nearest toilets, panic had started to set in. I alerted a nearby steward, who uttered a few words into a walkie-talkie. Thankfully, the drama was over no sooner than it had begun.

The concourse below us ran the length of the Sir Alex Ferguson Stand, forming a wide corridor, segregated by a few fire doors which remained open on matchdays. With the second half under way, the half-time queues for the toilets and food and drink had cleared, leaving me with a near-unobstructed view to the far end of the corridor. There, in the distance, I caught a glimpse of him standing side-on, gazing up at a sign above one of the stairwells. I approached, quickly abandoning any attempts to ask what he'd been doing when I realised how disorientated he was. As per usual, he'd gone to the toilet at the interval, then, somehow, got lost in trying to find his way back. Slowly, I ushered him back towards his seat.

In mid-April, my mum had taken him for his scheduled hospital appointment with the oncologist, which had seemed to go well enough. His PSA reading had risen slightly, but not enough to cause any major concern. The cancer, he was told, was still in check, and provided he had no further issues, he wouldn't be seen for another few months. That had been a relief.

Nevertheless, I kept a close eye on him at the four games we went to together. Sevilla had been the third of them. After he got lost on the concourse, I decided it was best to follow him at half-time in the next match, maintaining just enough distance so he didn't suss what I was up to. On the whole, though, he'd seemed to be coping. Chris continued to assume the role of matchday taxi driver, dropping us off and picking us up close by Old Trafford to minimise Dad's time on his feet. He remained quiet throughout each game, going out of his way to avoid conversations, but that, I accepted, was the best I could hope for. The others around us had also got the message, limiting their interactions with him to pleasant hellos and goodbyes.

After the win over Arsenal in late April, I renewed my season ticket, convincing myself as I filled out the form that it was the right thing to do. Without him ever having or *wanting* to tell me, I knew that Dad had not renewed.

Dad saw Manchester United play in the flesh for the final time in May. A long time ago, back when he'd been healthy and active, I'd imagined that when the day eventually came, the game might be an important one and we'd have reason to remember it for something more than it being his last. Perhaps it would be a cup final down at Wembley or maybe a title decider, I'd hoped. But no. Disappointingly, it came to pass that Dad's 64-year stint as a match-going supporter was rounded off with a strong contender for the most meaningless competitive game of football he'd ever witnessed: an end-of-season dead rubber against Watford.

Even mathematically, the league had been over for a month. City had finally been confirmed champions when soon-to-be relegated West Brom had turned up at Old Trafford and nabbed a 1-0 win in the middle of April. The only crumb of comfort had been that United had avoided the ignominy of seeing City crowned champions the week before, when the second derby of the season had been held at the Etihad. A win would have done it for City and their owners had spared no expense at the prospect of rubbing United's noses in it like never before by lining the stadium roof with a lavish firework display, primed and ready to go after full time. City went two up before half-time, but United somehow clawed their way back level after the interval thanks to a couple of Paul Pogba goals. With the home crowd growing agitated at United's unexpected response, Chris Smalling volleyed what proved to be the winner. The inevitable was merely delayed, but the firework show was off, at least.

After West Brom, United did enough to ensure Champions League qualification and that they'd finish second. The league, then, was done, as was Europe. The only hope that the season might end on a high had come in the FA Cup, where United were due to play the final against Chelsea at Wembley the following weekend. That was the focus now, and therefore added to the insignificance of the Watford game.

Chris had picked me up two hours before kick-off. Ten minutes later we'd mounted the kerb outside Dad's. The afternoon was already warm, the sky near cloudless, yet Dad, perhaps out of habit, had draped an old, plucked scarf over his shoulders by the time he emerged from the front door. With a wince, he'd lowered himself into the passenger seat, grunting a quiet acknowledgement to us both as he yanked the seat belt towards the buckle.

5 *Live Sport* was on the radio, running through its previews of the final round of Premier League games for the season. Nobody in the car spoke as we pulled away. Chris twisted the volume dial up slightly to mask the silence. There, in the back seat, came the first pang of sadness. I thought back to a year earlier, when, on a similarly sunny day, Dad and I had stopped off at the pub on the way home and chatted for an hour over our end-of-season pint. I remembered his defiant words about how he wouldn't begin to consider giving up going to the football until he'd taken his grandson to a game. That, I knew now, would never happen, nor would we ever mark the finish of a season with a quiet pint. To think the chapter could close in such underwhelming fashion, on an afternoon both us wanted out of the way as soon as possible, was shit.

Off the M602, the traffic soon grew heavy. We limped through Trafford Park at a pace so agonisingly slow that I wondered if we'd make kick-off. Finally on Wharfside Way, we pulled level with one of the entrance gates to the stadium, where, with the traffic crawling towards a set of lights, Chris snapped an indicator on and the car came to a halt. Dad took a while to limber up from his position in the front, leaning against the car as he steadied himself on the pavement. Oblivious to the impatient dickhead in the BMW behind us, who felt the need to sound his horn, Dad joined me as we crossed the road, then the large canal bridge leading towards the Sir Alex Ferguson Stand.

Before reaching the queues for the lift came a flash of Dad's humour, which by then rarely surfaced. As recently as the start of the previous season, we'd complete a lap of the outside of the stadium before passing through the turnstiles. I don't know when it started but it had become part of the pre-game ritual long ago.

'Do you want to go straight in or shall we do a lap?' he'd asked, wryly. I didn't answer.

Out of the lift, we made directly for the seats, not bothering to stop for a programme. This wasn't a day worth remembering. With the temperature warm, the rest of the regulars came up from the concourse earlier than they would have done normally and stood chatting by their seats. Owed partly to the nothingness of the game, the atmosphere was pleasant, devoid of any final-day tension.

Before kick-off, Michael Carrick, appearing for a final time as a Manchester United player, was given an ovation and a guard of honour as he came out of the tunnel with his kids. The match began, understandably lacking in tempo.

The only goal came just after half an hour. I don't remember it, but footage reveals it began with Carrick floating a pass over the top of the Watford defence for Juan Mata, who had timed his run immaculately. His control instant, he squared a pass for Marcus Rashford, who applied the finish. That, I *think*, was the last goal Dad ever saw, but I can't be certain he *did* see it. Our seats were higher than the roof of the South Stand opposite us. That, coupled with the large sloping roof of our stand, created a huge rectangular window which looked out southwards, first over Stretford and the cricket ground and then, in the distance, out across part of the Cheshire Plain. On clear days you could easily pick out planes taking off and coming in to land at the airport. Several times I'd glanced at Dad; on each occasion his eyes had been gazing out of the stadium, mind somewhere else.

Half-time came and went. I spent it following him in and out of the toilets, making sure he remembered his way back, which he did without intervention. The second half passed without goals or anything I can recall that was even vaguely exciting. Dad sat back, arms folded, scarf still hanging over his shoulders, waiting for the full-time whistle.

As is routinely the way after the last full time of the season, there wasn't the usual mass scramble for the exits as soon as the game finished. Instead, the majority simply stood and waited for a few words from the manager and to bid farewell to those players who may be moving on. The team began a lap of appreciation, with pockets of the more vocal supporters serenading them with songs about the imminent visit to Wembley.

As soon as the last of the players had passed us on the pitch below, the handshakes and goodbyes began all around us, the air quickly filling with the usual 'see you in August' and 'have a great summer'.

Dad had tried to hide his tears at this point. But by the time Frank and Nige and Sue and Dave and all the other matchday friends he'd made over the years – even those whose faces we recognised but whose names we never learnt – had started to say their goodbyes, he could no longer disguise it. The tears streamed from him like I'd never seen before – more than after the Martial goal at Wembley; *much* more than during the minute's silence before Huddersfield. But it was the noise that accompanied them which was by far the worst part. It was incomparable to anything I'd ever heard from him: a long, drawn-out wail, punctuated by sharp, deep intakes of breath; the cry of a child, yet coming from a man in his 70s.

Awkwardly, I put an arm around his shoulders in an attempt to comfort him. He cupped his hands over his face and continued to sob. Realising this would not pass quickly, I pulled down his chair for him so we could sit in our seats for a final time. We stayed there for some time, watching the crowds drain out of the stadium. Eventually, he intimated he was ready, and carefully pulled himself to his feet. He was trembling when he stood up and reached for my hand as we headed towards the top of the steps down towards the exit. This was it: the end. Twenty-five years after he'd led me into Old Trafford by the hand for my first game, here I was, leading him by his as he departed for a final time. At the top of the steps, he grasped the handrail and began to descend, giving no final glance back at the pitch as he went.

That moment and the sound of his cry had kept me awake that night. A week later, it was still on my mind as, for the first time in my life, I made the journey down to Wembley without him. Out of habit, I stuck to the usual route and itinerary: setting off early to beat the rush of traffic on the M6, stopping at the same service stations. I even had dinner in the same place, before catching the tube in good time to take in the atmosphere on Wembley Way.

The game itself was an enormous disappointment. Lukaku wasn't fit to start. Neither was Marouane Fellaini, who missed out altogether, denying United their two most physically imposing players. After 20 minutes, Phil Jones was caught leaden-footed when Cesc Fàbregas played a pass towards Eden Hazard on halfway. Hazard's first touch allowed him to scamper clear and into the penalty area. Jones had appeared to catch him up, but, with the angle for a shot narrowing, his attempt to prod the ball out for the corner saw him bring him down for a penalty. Hazard kept his head to stroke it home.

From there, there was an inevitability to it all. Chelsea, Antonio Conte's Chelsea for a final time, would be content to sit deep and play defensively, knowing United lacked the kind of physical threat in their attack to pose them too much trouble. This was largely the way it went, though there were chances after half-time: Alexis Sánchez had an equaliser struck off for straying marginally offside; Paul Pogba mistimed a free header from a corner late on. Chelsea hung on.

I didn't wait around for the trophy lift, leaving soon after the whistle to try and beat the rush at Wembley Park station. Seeing your team lose at Wembley is never nice, but things become markedly worse when you live at the other end of the country and have to be back that same night – something those who schedule the kick-off times never seem to give much thought to. Eventually I made it to the platform as the sun was beginning to dip in the sky, feeling thoroughly miserable and dreading the prospect of a six-hour motorway slog back up north.

I pulled out my phone and tried to call Dad. He didn't pick up. I'd missed him. Going to watch your team play in a big final is as much about the rest of the day as it is the game itself. Winning those finals becomes more memorable, more special, when you're with someone you care about, just as losing them becomes more tolerable.

There, waiting for my train, I regretted my decision to renew my season ticket for the first time.

Chapter 6

The curse of Belgrade

DAD HAD a friend through school. I can't remember his name or if he ever told me it to begin with, but in the years before Munich, he'd been a regular member of the gang that caught the morning train on matchdays. He'd lived in one of the terraced houses somewhere on the other side of the railway bridge to the pub, and would knock for Dad before the pair of them made their way up the steps to the platform to meet the others.

After the crash, though, the boy stopped. The enormity of what happened left such irreparable scars that returning to Old Trafford was simply too painful for him to face. Initially, Dad and the others had assumed his absence was only a temporary thing, but as the months rolled on it became apparent it wasn't. Never, in the time Dad knew the boy, did he go back to see a game.

There were a few others from outside of Dad's friendship circle who had made the same decision – familiar faces often seen on matchdays, that, from that day in February 1958, weren't seen again. Dad understood it. For a time after attending his first game back against Forest the day after Duncan died, he'd considered taking a similar approach. He was 14 the month after Munich and *playing* football was beginning to eat into more and more of his free time than ever before. Scouts from various professional clubs had taken an interest in him, with some offering trials. Perhaps there were other ways to channel his passion for the sport without having to be constantly reminded of the tragedy which befell the team he adored.

Relatively quickly he realised he couldn't turn his back on it. Too much of his young life had already been taken up by them to justify making a clean break. He accepted it couldn't be the same as it was before, but giving it up wasn't something he'd be able to do, even if he tried. Into the spring, after the initial shock had dulled, he found that being back among the crowd at games had been comforting. The familiarity of the sights and the sounds and the smells had felt like the best place for him to be to work through the grief.

Following the initial surge of support for the team following the crash, attendances dropped off towards the end of the season as United's patched-up side went on a long, winless run at home in the league. Dad was aware of the decline in numbers on the terraces, but, after what had happened, he felt an obligation to keep going. He realised that his need to be there had grown stronger than ever. This desire culminated in him making his first trip to Wembley that May, something he managed to accomplish without his parents finding out – or so he thought.

While United managed just one more win in the league in the 1957/58 season, they followed their FA Cup win over Sheffield Wednesday a fortnight after Munich by defeating West Brom in a quarter-final replay, setting up a semi-final with Fulham in late March. The first meeting ended in a 2-2 draw at Villa Park but, again, United were victorious in the replay, winning 5-3 at Highbury. Miraculously, Jimmy Murphy had guided them to the final.

The exact details of Dad's Wembley debut were always a little bit sketchy. The story went that there had been another

boy in school who occasionally went along to games with
Dad's gang. He hadn't been a regular and he and Dad hadn't
ever been particularly close. The boy's father, though, had
some form of connection with the club through his job, and
was able to acquire some tickets for the final. Knowing Dad
to be an avid fan, the boy had unexpectedly approached him
at the bus stop one morning before school and presented him
with an offer he couldn't possibly turn down. He could have
a ticket, the boy told him, and was welcome to travel down
with him and his father, staying in the same accommodation
when in London. Dad didn't hesitate. He agreed in an instant,
despite knowing there wasn't a cat in hell's chance his parents
– particularly his mother – would ever consent to it.

Allowing himself a couple of days' thinking time, he
formulated a plan. He told his parents he would be spending
the weekend of the final at one of the nearby farms owned by
the family of another friend. With summer approaching the
air was warm enough for them to camp out among a small
wooded area on the far side of their farmland, well away from
the road and railway line. They agreed to it without asking
too many questions and he'd been surprised at how easily they
bought the lie. On the Friday, he'd embarked on a long train
journey down to London.

United faced Bolton Wanderers in the final. Matt Busby,
having finally been released from hospital the previous
month, watched on from the Wembley stands as Murphy led
the team out. United had donned new shirts for the game,
each featuring the image of a phoenix on the club crest. The
symbolism was obvious, but, disappointingly for Dad, this
was not the day United rose from their ashes.

Simply reaching the final had been an incredible feat,
but hopes they might go one better were swiftly dashed as
Nat Lofthouse opened the scoring inside three minutes.
United created several opportunities to draw level – the best

of which came when Bobby Charlton thumped a shot against the inside of the Bolton post – but an equaliser eluded them. Early in the second half, Lofthouse scored again, putting Bolton firmly in command of the game. There was a touch of controversy to it. Dennis Stevens's shot had been struck firmly at Harry Gregg in the United goal. He'd palmed the ball up into the air and turned quickly to catch it before it dropped over the line. Just as he attempted to gather the ball, Lofthouse steamed in, clattering into him and bundling the ball into the goal in the process. Nowadays it would have been blown up as a foul, but in 1958 goalkeepers weren't afforded the same level of protection. Gregg remained on the floor as Lofthouse and the other Bolton players celebrated. Despite a few half-hearted appeals from United defenders, the goal was permitted to stand. That was the end of the scoring.

Dad returned home late on the Sunday afternoon. His father had been in the room behind the bar area when he arrived and was quick to ask how his camping expedition had gone. Dad was careful to keep his answers short and vague, aware that too much detail might result in a slip which would reveal the truth. A few seconds passed and, confident he'd got away with it, Dad made for the stairs up to his bedroom.

'Shame about the final,' his father had called to him. Dad had turned to see the knowing, half smile on his face. No more was spoken of the final between them. It later dawned on him that the father of the boy who had provided him with the ticket drank in the pub on a semi-regular basis. He strongly suspected his dad had been in contact with him about the trip before the offer of a ticket had even been made and that he'd known exactly what was going on all along. He was certain his mum, on the other hand, had been oblivious to it, and so it was in the best interests of both of them that no more was ever said.

United's season didn't end at Wembley but a couple of weeks later, in Milan. United still had the European Cup semi-final they had reached in Belgrade the day before the crash. UEFA decided it would be unreasonable to expect United to fly for the away leg of the semi, and that this would be factored in when deciding their opponent. Ties with Real Madrid and Hungary's Vasas were ruled out, leaving United to face AC Milan. Dad went to the first leg at Old Trafford, where United came from a goal down to win 2-1. A week later they were crushed 4-0 in the San Siro, after travelling there by land and sea.

The loss proved to be United's last appearance in the European Cup for over seven years. UEFA, in a gesture born out of sympathy for what had happened, had offered them the chance to enter the competition the following season only for the Football League to intervene. Thwarted in their previous attempts to block United entering the European Cup, they pointed out United were no longer English champions, thus ineligible.

Later that same year, my grandparents sold the pub, moving a couple of miles down the road to the village of Culcheth. Dad had been devastated to leave but, between his final years of school and playing and watching football as much as he did, he barely had time to dwell on it. Crucially to him, a new family home hadn't interfered much with his football. After playing on Saturday mornings, he still had ample time to change and make his way to Old Trafford in time for a three o'clock kick-off every other week. That, as he approached his late teens, was all that really mattered to him.

The early years of United's rebuild were difficult times. Busby made his return as manager the next season. After finally being discharged from hospital and passed fit enough to resume work, he continued to suffer with excruciating pain in his back and leg – a legacy of the crash. The mental toll had also been significant: he was tormented by survivor's guilt after the crash, telling family and loved ones how he had felt personally responsible for the loss of life having insisted on taking his team into European football in the first place. His wife Jean had urged him to continue as manager to honour the memory of those who had died. This had been enough to persuade him, but he knew restoring United to the force they had been would be a long road.

Quickly replacing those who had been lost was impossible. Although Busby had shown he had no qualms with putting his faith in young players, the circumstances they faced were unprecedented. Even the most talented would be weighed down by the pressure of striving for the obscenely high standards set by their predecessors.

United overachieved in their first full season after Munich, finishing second. Bobby Charlton, still grappling with his own deep-running grief after the loss of so many of his friends, finished the campaign as the top scorer with 29 goals.

United's decline became more obvious from there, finishing the next two seasons seventh before dropping to 15th in 1961/62. In terms of the league, the next season was even worse. Despite the high-profile signing of Denis Law from Torino, United plummeted to 19th, avoiding relegation by only two points. Yet despite their brush with a drop to the second tier, the end of that season brought a turning point in the shape of an unexpected FA Cup win.

United reached the final against a Leicester City that had finished fourth in the league, at one stage looking favourites to win the championship. A late dip in form during the final weeks of the season had cost them and perhaps weighed on their players' minds as Law gave United the lead after half an hour of the final. David Herd doubled United's advantage with the hour approaching, only for Leicester to halve the deficit with ten minutes left. Any United nerves were eased soon after, when Herd scored his second, restoring the two-goal cushion and sealing a 3-1 win. That victory was a springboard for United at a time when they – and Busby – had badly needed it.

Ahead of the 1963/64 season, there was optimism that United were on the right track after all and not as far away from re-establishing themselves as a major force as their league position had suggested. Busby was continuing to shape his side. Following Law's arrival, he'd bolstered his midfield with the signing of Paddy Crerand from Celtic in the February before the cup run. Collyhurst-born Nobby Stiles began to play regularly, adding extra bite in midfield. These three players would go on to play key roles as United clambered back towards the summit of English football, the team continuing to evolve over the next 12 months.

A hint of what was to come came in September, during an early season home game against West Brom when Busby had given a surprise start to a 17-year-old Belfast-born winger by the name of George Best.

If Dad was there to see Best make his debut – and he probably *was* – he certainly didn't remember it. I know this now because, wrongly, he often told me about watching Best make his first-team bow a whole three months later, in a game against Burnley which took place on a bitterly cold afternoon during the Christmas period.

On Boxing Day of 1963, Dad had got himself up to Turf Moor, where he saw United play terribly and come away with a deserved 6-1 battering. He was livid and so too was Busby, who responded by making changes before the next game, which, because all clubs played back-to-back fixtures against local teams in the Christmas week around that time, saw United host Burnley at Old Trafford.

Best had dropped back into the reserves after his actual debut back in September but was named a starter. Playing on the left wing, he scored his first senior goal in a 5-1 win, tormenting Burnley's defenders for the duration.

Perhaps he wasn't quite as dominant on the day as some make out, but Best, skinny frame drowning in a red shirt which looked at least one size too big for him, undoubtedly produced a display which was enough for most in attendance to leave with the impression he had the potential to be something special.

Dad, mildly stunned at the fact he was a couple of years older than Best, was almost immediately convinced he was on the path for the very top. By then he had already seen his fair share of pacy wingers in a United shirt, but Best stood out. His close control when travelling at speed was phenomenal, keeping the ball under his spell even when it unexpectedly bobbled up off the uneven playing surface. In the tighter areas of the pitch, where open space was at a premium and he couldn't rely exclusively on a burst of acceleration to beat a man, his ability to swivel his hips and shift direction so easily proved lethal to defenders trying to remain upright on a pitch tested by the depths of a harsh Mancunian winter.

It came so naturally and Dad had been reminded of watching Duncan in the early days. The two were very different – both in physical stature and playing styles – but there was a familiar feeling to witnessing the ease with which a teenager took to the men's game.

On the night Best died in 2005, Dad stayed up into the small hours of the morning. Sipping from a glass of whiskey, he told me how watching him that afternoon was one of his fondest memories at Old Trafford, a small reward for persevering with the gloom of the five years preceding it. Best steadily began to establish himself as a permanent fixture from that day forward. Before long, he was combining devastatingly with Charlton and Law. United's first team ended the 1963/64 season without a trophy, but they shot to second in the league. Another sign that an exciting new era lay ahead came from the youth team, which claimed United their first FA Youth Cup since 1957. Best scored in the final against Swindon Town.

After a slow start to the next season, United picked up form. By the spring it was clear that United or Don Revie's Leeds would be champions. In April, United won 1-0 in a crucial encounter at Elland Road thanks to a goal from John Connelly. From there, Busby's side got over the line, finishing level on points with Leeds but with a better goal average. For the first time since 1957 they were English champions.

As United basked in the glow of their league glory that summer, Dad was 21 and nearing the end of his time training to become a PE teacher. He'd drifted a little through the years since leaving school, not really knowing what he wanted to do with his life. At some point he'd reluctantly abandoned ambitions of a professional football career when his parents pressured him into rejecting the chance to sign for Blackburn Rovers, where he'd impressed during a trial. Football, to their way of thinking, wasn't something you could realistically do as a well-paid job and, influenced by their own experiences of running the pub, they urged him to pursue a career in hotel management. At 18 he'd left home for Sheffield where he worked in a city-centre hotel as part of a training programme, despising every second of it and failing to see out the first six months.

After returning home, his father pulled some strings to find him a temporary job in the painting department at a local civil engineering firm until he could enrol for teacher training at Padgate College in Warrington.

It turned out well enough for him. Money saved from the time he spent working helped him afford his first car, a second-hand Ford Anglia, which he adored. Owning a car meant he was no longer reliant on trains and buses to get to and from United games. His studies allowed him to play more football than ever before. In the week he represented Padgate's first team, who, despite facing teams from bigger, more prestigious universities, had been extremely competitive around that time. His weekends free, he began playing for Nantwich Town in the Manchester League, occasionally missing out on watching United to do so.

By then, the gang with whom he'd attended so many games in his youth had scattered. One or two of them would occasionally join him for the odd match but, possibly exacerbated by United's decline, other things like jobs and partners and the need to save up and buy houses had taken precedence over seeing the team play every other Saturday afternoon. Dad was pleased he'd seen it through to witness United win the league again. Knowing he'd gone the distance and barely missed a home game to reach that moment had made it doubly sweet.

The focus had, however, quickly shifted. Being crowned champions of England again was significant, of course, but conquering Europe the next season represented something far greater than the trophy. Not only had they secured their place in the competition, there was a strong sense that the crop of players Busby had at his disposal was good enough to win it.

As had become something of a pattern around that era, United made a slow start to the domestic season, winning 1-0 against Sheffield Wednesday on the first day of the league, then losing to Nottingham Forest and drawing their next three games. Their inconsistent form continued through September, up to an eagerly anticipated European Cup preliminary round tie with HJK Helsinki. Playing in Finland in the first leg, United won 3-2, then cruised to a 6-0 victory in the return. They were on their way.

Before the year was out, United swept aside Vorwärts Berlin in the first round, putting themselves in a commanding position with a 2-0 win in the first leg in Germany before finishing the job with a 3-1 success at Old Trafford. That result teed up their sternest test to date: a quarter-final against Benfica.

The scale of the task facing them was enormous. In United's absence from the European Cup, Benfica had established themselves as one of the dominant forces, winning the competition in 1961 and 1962. Their attack spearheaded by the great Eusébio, they'd never been beaten at home in a European fixture. With the first leg hosted at Old Trafford, it was imperative United took a lead with them to Lisbon – ideally a comfortable one.

It started disastrously. José Augusto had given Benfica a lead inside the first ten minutes and Dad, who had been in the thick of the Stretford End that night, had feared the worst. United had been nervy for a spell after the goal. Gradually, though, things began to turn as they settled and started to create opportunities. With half-time in sight, came the response: Herd levelled and, with Old Trafford rocking, Law added a second just before the break. They continued on the front foot after half-time and were duly rewarded when Foulkes added a third with half an hour to play. Benfica came back, perhaps sensing a two-goal deficit would be too much to overcome in Lisbon. José Torres scored late on to pull it back to 3-2. United had a lead, but a precarious one.

The second leg was played in early March and proved to be one of the great nights in United's history, as they roared to the kind of victory which had been completely unthinkable prior to kick-off. Much of the damage was done within the opening 15 minutes by Best, who, on that night, truly announced himself on the world stage.

Still only 19, his status in the UK had risen sharply in the two years since his first goal against Burnley. His ability coupled with his good looks meant he was already beginning to transcend the sport from which he earned a living. In Lisbon that night, it reached another dimension.

With six minutes on the clock, United won a free kick midway through the Benfica half, which Tony Dunne floated into the penalty area. Best timed his run and leap perfectly, guiding his header into the far corner of the goal. Minutes later, with Benfica still reeling from Best's opener, Herd, back to goal, nodded down a long punt downfield from Harry Gregg. It dropped between two Benfica players who, for a fraction of a second, hesitated as they each expected the other to deal with it. Best pounced on their indecision, driving forward. His first touch took him clear of the two opponents, his second saw him glide beyond a leaden-footed third and into the area. There, he angled a shot beyond the goalkeeper, into the far corner.

Benfica were shellshocked. This simply didn't happen to them. Before they had time to fully process what was going on, Connelly made it three.

A Shay Brennan own goal saw Benfica pull one back in the second half, but a comeback never really felt possible. United, completely undaunted by their surroundings, continued to play with their tails up. Crerand added a fourth. Then, as stoppage time approached, Charlton walked in another to complete the scoring. More than 1,000 miles away, Dad pinched himself as he tuned a radio to listen to the final minutes.

An emphatic 5-1 win over one of the best teams around. This, surely, was United's time. Destiny was calling.

But no.

United were paired with Partizan Belgrade in the semi, teeing up an emotional return to the scene of the last game played by the Babes. There, in the first leg, they fell to a shock

2-0 defeat. Best had played but, suffering with a cartilage problem, looked a shadow of the player who had sliced through Benfica. Busby had known about the injury before the game, but aware of the psychological boost it would give the opposition were Best to miss out, he persuaded his star to play with a strapping round his knee. Best had aggravated it before the match was over, effectively ending his season.

Before his injury and with the score still 0-0, Best managed to lay on a chance for Law to give United the lead inside the first half, only for the Scot to turn the ball on to the bar from two yards. The miss would come back to haunt United as two second-half Partizan goals left them with a mountain to climb in the second leg at Old Trafford.

By the time of the second leg, United's hopes of retaining their league title were all but over after a flurry of poor results. Failure to overturn the deficit would mean a wait of at least another year before re-entering the European Cup, which heaped even more pressure on before kick-off.

In Best's absence, United dominated the possession and chances, swarming Partizan from the first whistle but failing to score. Their flow was disrupted when Crerand and one of the Partizan players were sent off for fighting but a breakthrough eventually came late in the game, courtesy of Nobby Stiles. That, though, was the end of the scoring. Partizan survived a late onslaught. They – not United – advanced to the final.

The United dressing room had been silent at full time. Busby, having come so tantalisingly close to finally delivering his team to the final, had tears in his eyes. A few yards away at around that time, Dad filtered out of one of the gates at the back of the Stretford End. Immediately outside stood the tower of one of the floodlights, set back a few of yards from the ground itself. The sense of frustration had seen a scrap break out between supporters as they tried to squeeze through the narrow passage between the stand and the floodlight tower. Fortunately, a policeman with a whistle was on hand to intervene and disperse those involved before it became ugly. The bitter disappointment was palpable as Dad trudged away. United had missed their chance. Victory in Europe, it seemed, would be forever out of their grasp.

Chapter 7

Bad news

FRANK AND I stood up as the half-time whistle sounded, waiting for the usual rush towards the concourse to ease before retaking our seats. It was November 2018. United were on their way to a goalless draw with Crystal Palace on one of those now all-too-rare occasions when they'd been granted a 3pm kick-off on a Saturday.

Winter was tightening its grip again. The greyness of the afternoon was rapidly giving way to darkness and, on the other side the pitch, the row of floodlights lining the roof of the South Stand grew brighter in the increasing gloom. A small band of ground staff emerged on the grass below, prodding at the playing surface with their pitchforks, working any small pieces of turf that had come loose back into place. As I watched one of the men tend to an area close to the touchline immediately in front of us, Frank, arms folded, turned towards me and asked the same question he'd asked every single half-time since the season started.

'How's he getting on then?' he said, and, with barely a pause, I reeled off the same kind of vague response I gave every other time he'd asked.

'Yeah, he's fine,' I lied, pushing out the standard small talk response. 'Not really doing that much with himself, but he's getting by.'

'Tell him I've been asking after him, won't you?' Frank followed up, and I assured him I would. That, usually, was where the conversation ended or moved on to something else, but not this time.

'Look,' Frank continued. 'I'll be going away on holiday in January and I'm missing a couple of games. If he wants my ticket for either of them, tell him he can have it. I'll leave it with you before I go. No need to pay me.'

I nodded along and thanked him for his generous offer, resisting the urge to tell him that there was no way we'd be taking him up on it. Frank had cast a quick glance across the pitch and again I falsely assumed the conversation was done.

'We've really missed him this season,' he added, and upon hearing that I'd felt my bottom lip begin to tremble. I turned my face away and tugged my scarf up over my mouth until the impulse to cry passed. Frank, though, had twigged something was amiss. From the corner of my eye, I saw that he'd quickly looked back at me as I pulled at my scarf. There was little point keeping it a secret.

'Actually,' I began, 'we've had some bad news.'

* * *

After the disappointment of the FA Cup Final at Wembley at the end of May, I hadn't seen much of Dad over the summer. The World Cup and England's unanticipated run to the semi-finals in Russia ensured I remained extremely busy with work. Days off were spent largely with Ethan who, having not long since learnt to walk, made certain they were anything but restful.

August had come around soon enough, and the new season began with a 2-1 win against Leicester on a balmy Friday evening at Old Trafford. For the first time in over six months, I walked the familiar route: leaving the car on the old multi-storey on the edge of Media City, crossing the foot bridge and turning up Elevator Road towards Wharfside Way for the final approach to the ground. When I arrived, there was almost an entire hour to kill before kick-off and so, recalling Dad's joke before the Watford game back in May, I completed a lap at a leisurely pace.

The place was already heaving by then, particularly outside the East Stand, where the more touristy elements of the fanbase posed for photographs and spilled out of the megastore clutching bags of club merchandise and freshly printed replica shirts. Occasionally, a song broke out, usually from small groups of supporters who'd spent a good chunk of the afternoon in a pub. More often than not, those hours before a new season begins are sacred for football supporters, a time to look forward, not back, and any residual negativity from the previous season or frustrations at an underwhelming transfer window can be forgotten as you convince yourself that the season to come will be one to remember for the right reasons.

This time though, I was aware that possibly for the first time since football had meant something to me, I didn't share the same giddy sense of anticipation with my fellow match-goers. In truth, I'd been dreading going back to Old Trafford all summer. The second half of the previous season had provided me with plenty of opportunities to grow accustomed to watching games without Dad beside me, but I'd yet to experience a match with someone else in *his* seat. I loathed the thought of arriving to see a stranger sitting there, knowing nothing about the previous occupant or the years upon years of memories tied to it.

As August approached, it was on my mind more and more. I hoped that, miraculously, there would be some sort of mix-up at the ticket office and the seat would remain empty. Knowing deep down that this was impossible, I told myself the best outcome would be if it wasn't allocated to another season ticket holder. I could just about cope with seeing *different* people in Dad's seat every other week, but the idea of it belonging to a *single* person – someone I'd inevitably have to see and speak to regularly – made me feel uneasy.

Because of this, I left it as late as I could before entering, minimising the potential for awkward interactions. I arrived at my seat just in time to see the teams filing out of the tunnel, shaking hands and trading brief hellos with the regulars as I sidestepped down the row. Sure enough, Dad's seat had been taken. A tall man said a polite hello and quickly followed up by asking if I was a season ticket holder. When I said that I was, he told me his name, which I didn't catch but think was Martin, and explained he'd be sitting next to me for the season to come.

'Yeah, I used to sit up in the top tier,' he went on. 'I've been after getting in this block for years.'

I held my tongue.

As the first few games passed, 'Martin', whose name I was never certain of, turned out to be a nice bloke and I felt foolish for spending so much of the summer worrying about who might take Dad's seat. He quickly fitted in with the other regulars and we soon discovered he could rival Nige when it came to launching withering attacks on referees at the slightest hint of a questionable decision. I never did tell him that his seat used to be Dad's but realised after the first few weeks that someone else had when he unexpectedly asked me how long I'd been coming to games with him.

After the Leicester win, United's season rapidly descended into chaos. Paul Pogba had helped France win the World Cup in Russia and, after all the talk of his fractured relationship with José Mourinho, became the subject of a relentless stream of speculation linking him to Real Madrid and Juventus. In the end he stayed, but United failed to significantly strengthen their squad around him, despite finishing so far off City.

Mourinho had been at his cantankerous best during much of pre-season, doing little to mask his displeasure at the lack of signings. When United lost consecutive games at Brighton and then at home to Spurs at the end of August, some of the fanbase had grown frustrated with him. From there, you knew what was coming. Mourinho's cycle as manager was approaching its end.

I'd driven down to Dad's house to watch the Brighton match on TV with him. While he wasn't able to be at the stadium in person now, I was determined to watch as many of the televised away games with him in the hope that it might help preserve a degree of normality. United were wretched from the off and were 3-1 down by half-time. As the first of the advert breaks came on, I'd turned to ask Dad if he wanted me to flick the kettle on only to realise he'd dozed off at some point in the minutes before half-time. I'd been too engrossed in the game to notice.

In early September we went on a family holiday for a week. Acutely aware of Dad's deterioration, I was keen to give him the chance to spend some quality time with Ethan, just in case things took another sharp dip before the end of the year. Dad continued to be at his most animated when Ethan came to visit, still making the effort to sit at the table with him on his lap and push along some of his Thomas the Tank Engine toys around with him. A week in each other's company would be good for them both, I thought.

Partly for sentimental reasons, we'd settled on Croatia. Dad had owned caravans as a young man and revelled in planning big driving holidays down into Europe. The long summer holiday he was afforded through teaching saw him go away for as long as a month at a time, usually down through the Black Forest in Germany and then on towards Bavaria or the Swiss Alps or even over the Brenner Pass and into Italy. In a time before satnav and the boom of budget airline flights, it was a great adventure for him – something which required weeks of meticulous planning. When I was a year old, Dad saw fit to embark on just about the longest journey of all, driving us down to what was then Yugoslavia. We'd stayed on a campsite close to the shores of Lake Bled for a few days before pressing on towards the coast and what would later become Croatia. Going back there three decades later with Ethan seemed like a nice idea.

We booked into a hotel on the outskirts of Dubrovnik, overlooking the mouth of a wide inlet through which the cruise ships passed to reach the city's harbour. Lauren and I had stayed in the same hotel a couple of years earlier when she was pregnant with Ethan, and so reassured my mum it would be perfect for Dad, who we imagined would want to spend most of his time watching his grandson play in the water from the edge of the kids' pool. If he was up to a walk, there was a small park immediately outside the hotel's front door with several benches strategically placed in the shade of several large pine trees. If he wanted food, there were a couple of nice restaurants and a shop on the other side of the parkland. Everything he needed was close by.

On the first day, though, Dad didn't make it out of his room. He'd felt unwell on the three-hour flight over from Manchester and needed to sleep it off, my mum told us. The second day he made it down for breakfast and half-heartedly picked at a plate of fruit my mum had brought him from the buffet table. After it, he perched on the edge of a sun lounger for an hour by the pool before it became too hot and he informed us he was going back to his room for a lie down. We didn't see him again that day. As the end of the week approached, we'd barely seen him for more than two hours of each day and my mum had grown increasingly concerned.

On the penultimate evening of the holiday, I knocked on the door of their room to see if they wanted to join us for a meal at one of the restaurants on the other side of the park. My mum answered and, over her shoulder, I saw that Dad was lying flat on the bed again, sleeping. My mum slipped out of the door, pulling it behind her so it was almost completely closed. Keeping her voice low, she told me she had decided to book him in at the doctor's as soon as she got back to England. There, in the darkness of the corridor, she said the word dementia for the first time.

Back home an appointment was hastily arranged, only for Dad – in typically stubborn fashion – to refuse to attend it. For a while there had been a slight improvement after the holiday. He appeared more content in the familiar surroundings of home and no longer needed to sleep for long periods of each day. My mum had doubted herself and wondered if she'd over-reacted to his behaviour on the holiday. Gradually though, as October arrived and the nights began to draw in, he started to regress once again. From late afternoon through to bedtime at around 11, he'd sit in silence in a chair by the window, eyes either closed or fixed on the TV. Any attempts by my mum to strike up conversation led nowhere and as the weeks went by her frustration began to build. It had come to a head one Saturday night when, after a particularly difficult couple of days, the last of Mum's patience seeped away.

'Why don't you say anything when I try and speak to you?' she'd yelled across the lounge, immediately regretting that she'd snapped.

At first, he didn't respond and she wondered if her question had even registered. Slowly, though, he had pulled himself up to the edge of his chair and leaned forward, cradling his head in his hands.

'I don't talk because I can't,' he said, stopping for a moment. 'I can't do it any more.'

The words had left his lips slowly, as if stringing so many together at once had taken genuine effort. It was the first time he acknowledged that he had a problem. The pair of them had wept.

Another appointment with a doctor was booked. This time, he attended. My mum accompanied him and called me late in the afternoon to fill me in on the details. Dad, the doctor suspected, was living with aphasia – a disorder caused by damage to parts of the brain responsible for the understanding and production of language. Usually, it comes about as the result of a stroke, but could also be caused by a progressive neurological condition, such as dementia. Dad would have to undergo a series of tests before a formal diagnosis was reached. When it was, he would likely have to undergo brain scans to determine the extent of the damage and, hopefully, learn more about what exactly was behind it.

Confusingly, hearing this news had kicked up a strong feeling of relief (which still doesn't feel like quite the right word). It was clearly upsetting, but the glimmer of clarity it brought had seemed to take the edge off it. At least, if we knew what it was, we could turn attention to dealing with it instead of drifting along with the uncertainty we'd lived with for at least the last 12 months. There was hope, too, that things might slightly improve with speech therapy once his diagnosis was confirmed, though the doctor had warned the chance of recovery was slimmer if the aphasia was a result of dementia.

Barely two weeks after absorbing this news, while raking together a sodden pile of leaves in the back yard one Wednesday afternoon, I'd felt my phone begin to buzz in my coat pocket. My mum was calling, and I instantly remembered why. Dad had been due for his appointment with the oncologist earlier that same day. Usually, on the morning of his appointments, I'd fire over a succinct text message wishing him well. He never once replied to any of them but I suppose it made me feel better to know I'd done it. On this occasion though, there had been no text. Probably because of the other stuff, his cancer appointment had totally slipped my mind.

As soon as I answered the call, I knew. Mum was crying hard on the other end of the line, her words were barely decipherable for the first few seconds and my heart began to pound as I tried to make sense of them. By her second or third attempt, I grasped what she was saying: the cancer had spread.

After it had risen marginally at his last appointment back in April, Dad's PSA reading had suddenly soared, a clear indicator that the cancer was no longer responding to treatment and beginning to thrive once again. Scans had been run, which had brought worse news: after 12 years, the cancer cells had escaped the prostate for the first time, taking hold in several lymph nodes in and around Dad's groin. There was a chance, the oncologist warned, that it could have migrated elsewhere, too. This would make matters far more complicated.

Dad had slumped forward in his chair when the news had been delivered, staring silently at the floor as my mum, fighting back tears, curled an arm around his shoulders. Without lifting his head, he had managed to compose himself enough to ask the important question: what next? He had two options: to embark on a final, aggressive course of chemotherapy or to do nothing and let the cancer take its natural course and make the most of the time he had left before it became unbearable.

'At this stage, it's a matter of whether you're willing to put your body through the chemo,' the oncologist added, almost as if trying to steer him towards the second option.

A small piece of paper with the telephone number for the oncologist's secretary written across it was passed to my mum. Dad was encouraged to take a few days to consider his decision and call after the weekend. He was adamant, however, that his mind was already made up.

'I want the chemo,' he told them.

The days that followed were difficult and filled with dark thoughts. For the first time since his initial cancer diagnosis all those years previously, the prospect of Dad dying soon felt very real again and I pondered how long he might have. Was it months, or was it now more appropriate to measure in weeks? There were moments when I'd also wonder if a rapid acceleration of the cancer's spread might, in some fucked-up kind of way, be the better alternative to him forgetting everyone and everything around him but going on to live a life of misery for another few years.

I'd built up some extra days of annual leave through work and was allowed to use them at short notice. Naturally, I felt compelled to spend as much time as I could with him. It was an international break that week, with England playing Croatia in a Nations League game at Wembley on the Sunday afternoon, only a few months after the World Cup semi-final defeat to the same opponents. Dad had never shown anywhere near the same level of enthusiasm for England as he had for United – neither of us had, in all honesty – but the opportunity to watch a match together while downing a couple of cans of beer was a welcome distraction given the misery of the circumstances.

England had ended up battling back from a goal down to win 2-1 – enough for them to clinch a place in arguably the most meaningless semi-final international football has to offer. Dad, as he had during the Brighton game, appeared close to sleep during one of the quieter spells of the first half. After barely putting together so much as three words, he had jolted into life shortly after England had equalised. Jesse Lingard scored the goal, and, when he realised this, Dad promptly pointed a finger at the TV and turned to me.

'Did you know that lad's from Warrington?' he asked. I did know, of course, but raised my eyebrows, as if the information he was sharing was new and interesting. 'I'm from there,' he added, like a boastful child, and a fresh wave of sadness exploded somewhere inside me.

I remembered how he'd been two years earlier, when Lingard's sweetly struck volley in extra time had won United the FA Cup Final against Crystal Palace. Lingard had grown up a short distance from Owen Street, where Dad's first home had stood. It had been a huge source of pride to him that a lad with such a close connection to where he'd been raised had scored such an important goal for his team. A few weeks after it, my parents had booked on to a cheap, last-minute deal to go on a cruise around Italy. Most of the others on the boat were Americans of around a similar age and not too well up on the happenings of English football. My mum had found it strange that whenever it came to introducing himself to one of the other passengers at one of the posh formal dinners they attended onboard every other night, Dad explained that he was from Warrington, without fail adding 'where Jesse Lingard is from'. This had prompted a few bemused looks and Mum later wondered if this was an early sign of the issues to come.

Chapter 8

1968

SHORTLY AFTER nine o'clock in the morning, after the last of the pupils had filed in through the entrances and taken their seats on the floor, the doors were closed and the hall had fallen silent. When it did, Dad, unshaven and eyes rimmed red from a lack of sleep, strode forward and took up a position at the front, wondering to himself as he did how he was supposed to get through the 15 minutes that lay ahead of him.

Usually, the assemblies at the school in Warrington where Dad had secured his first teaching position were taken by the headteacher or one of the other senior members of staff. On the occasions they weren't, there was a system in place whereby the rest of the teachers took it in turns to lead them. He'd been informed a week earlier that on the morning of Thursday, 30 May 1968 the responsibility would be his for the first time.

He was woefully unprepared. Having only arrived home at half past five that same morning, hands smeared with engine oil, he snatched little more than an hour of sleep before having to wake himself to get ready for work. He had only a vague idea of what he intended to say and so, over breakfast, scrawled some prompts on a piece of paper which, by the time he arrived at school, he realised he had left at home anyway.

As hundreds of pairs of eyes fell on him, he had been surprised at how calm he felt, the sleep deprivation seeming to stifle the nerves he had expected to have.

As a church-affiliated school, the assemblies were expected to carry a strong religious theme. There was always time for prayer at the end, but the rest of it was typically based around a scripture from the Bible which would contain some form of moral lesson for the pupils.

Dad, however, was never really a particularly religious man. Because of that, and because he was by now embracing the fact that he was completely winging his first full-school assembly, he took a bold, unconventional approach.

'Today,' he began, voice hoarse, 'I want to talk to you about Bobby Charlton and the European Cup Final.'

* * *

Dad was 23 years of age when he secured his first PE teaching job and couldn't believe how firmly he appeared to have landed on his feet. A teacher's wage was as modest in those days as it is today, but his first payslip had still been comfortably more money than he'd ever earned in one go. It didn't seem quite right, to his way of thinking, that he could be paid so handsomely for simply helping boys get better at sport.

Some of his wage had swiftly been lumped on a new car, his trusty Ford Anglia upgraded to a red (of course) Mini Cooper. After the car, the priority became saving for a house, which had very quickly become a necessity. Dad had a string of on-off, semi-serious girlfriends through his late teens and early 20s, each relationship fizzling out after a few months. At college, though, he'd met another girl and, by the time his training course approached its end, things had become more and more serious. The problem was that, unlike him, she wasn't local to Warrington. After college, it was likely she would have to return to her parents' house down on the south coast, which geography dictated would jeopardise the relationship. In a time where cohabiting was still by and large frowned upon, the obvious solution was marriage. Dad had proposed and, ever the romantic, had taken her to a game at Old Trafford as a means of celebration when she accepted.

His wedding day to his first wife was never an occasion either of us felt the need to discuss in any great detail. I know he was married in a church somewhere down where she was from and that, at the time, getting there felt like a voyage to a distant solar system to my grandmother, who had rarely strayed from a ten-mile radius of where she was born.

What was discussed, however, were the weeks prior to it, where Dad, in an almost boastful tone, would occasionally recall how little he had been fretting over his big day. Remaining faithful to his by then long-established priorities in life, his mind was instead taken up almost entirely with the fortunes of his football club as, finally, United homed in on their first European Cup Final.

The Partizan defeat in 1966 cut deep. At about the same time Dad was witnessing the policeman with the whistle breaking up the scrap at the back of the Stretford End, United's players had returned to the dressing room in the bowels of the South Stand, where they sat for the best part of an hour in disappointed silence. Busby could hardly bring himself to speak, but eventually uttered the words which had encapsulated what everyone connected with the club was feeling in that precise moment. 'We'll never win the European Cup now,' he sighed.

Another crack at the European Cup was, in the still of that unhappy dressing room, a long way off. Re-entry into the competition would only be granted by winning the league again. Picking his players up was to be a stern test of Busby's ability as a manager, particularly given the depth of his personal disappointment. At 57 and after over two decades as manager, it was reasonable to question if time might outrun him in his pursuit of continental glory.

He'd trusted the squad that came up short against Partizan to get them back into the European Cup. An overhaul of the squad wasn't necessary, the only major arrival that summer being goalkeeper Alex Stepney from Chelsea, after Harry Gregg had been blighted by injuries. A contractual dispute with Denis Law was also resolved and United were good to go.

In August, Dad had driven over the Pennines to Elland Road, where he saw them outplayed by Leeds, who won 3-1, casting instant doubt over whether Busby could guide them back to the top again. Although their home form was good, that defeat seemed to set the tone for their away performances, where they had lost their next three games on the spin. The last of those defeats had come at Nottingham Forest on 1 October, but was followed by an eight-game unbeaten run, when only Chelsea had taken a point from them. Two more defeats away to Aston Villa and Sheffield United came in December, but that was it; a run which began the day after Boxing Day saw them go the remainder of the league season without a single defeat.

Had they not drawn nearly all of their away matches throughout this period, they might have had the league title sewn up far earlier than they did. As it went, United knew a win in their penultimate game of the season, away to West Ham, would clinch the championship. They finished the job in style with an emphatic 6-1 win.

Becoming champions again, though, was of course only part of it. Unlocking the door to Europe had seemed to matter more than reclaiming their status as England's best team. A United side still very much in their prime would get another chance in the European Cup.

A week after the West Ham game, Dad had taken his dad with him to see United presented with the First Division trophy at their final home match of the season – a drab goalless draw with Stoke. Though he was responsible for introducing Dad to matchdays at Old Trafford all those years earlier, my grandad never possessed anything close to the same obsessive level of interest in football as his son. He *appreciated* it as a sport and enjoyed attending the odd game, but it was clear to Dad from a young age that it wasn't something he was ever truly passionate about.

As a young man, my grandad had been a talented cricketer and excelled as a wicketkeeper. There had been talk, I think, of representing Lancashire at one stage, though it failed to materialise. Later in life, when he'd eventually stopped playing cricket, he'd spend many a summer afternoon at the other Old Trafford, watching Lancashire or the occasional England Test.

Unexpectedly, my grandad's interest in football had spiked dramatically in the mid-1960s. Suddenly he had developed a strange desire to accompany Dad to United games on a regular basis. It wasn't *every* match – probably more like one in three – but certainly more frequently than ever before. At the time, Dad hadn't questioned it all that much. He wrongly assumed, he would tell me sometime after my grandad died, that it was to do with George Best, whose allure had seemed to pull in scores of new faces to Old Trafford every single matchday around that time. Approaching his 60th birthday by then, my grandad had appeared to get swept up in the excitement and would speak enthusiastically about how much he enjoyed seeing Best run with the ball.

Twenty years or so later, after my grandad was diagnosed with Parkinson's Disease and had to be moved into a nursing home, my grandmother had confessed that the real motivation had actually been to spend time with his son. Dad's life had steadily become more busy. His teacher training had swallowed up the bulk of his time; the rest had been divided between his fiancée and playing and watching football at weekends. Time in his parents' company had seemed to diminish with every passing month and his dad had felt this more keenly than anyone else in the family. Going to United, he came to realise, would give them two or three hours in each other's company they wouldn't otherwise have had.

Dad was still playing for Nantwich at the start of the 1967/68 season. That, for the first time since he was ten, had meant he wasn't able to make the majority of United's home games in the league during that season. This hadn't seemed to matter quite as much as it would have done in previous years as, for him, the entire season had revolved around the European matches, played in the middle of the week. He and my grandad went to all of them together, something he would say made what happened all the more special.

The first round was a canter. United put four unanswered goals past Hibernians of Malta in the first leg at Old Trafford in September, then finished the job with a goalless draw in the away leg a week later. That had teed up a second-round meeting with FK Sarajevo, where, for the final few moments of the second leg, Dad wondered if nerves might force him to projectile vomit across a packed Stretford End.

The away leg in Bosnia had come before the game at Old Trafford and finished 0-0. United were clear favourites to progress with the home crowd behind them but, perhaps fuelled by memories of Partizan, Dad felt strangely uneasy in the couple of hours before kick-off. His nerves had been calmed early on when the Sarajevo goalkeeper parried a headed effort along his line and John Aston darted forward to stab the ball into the goal. It remained 1-0 until the middle of the second half and the apprehension had slowly crept back in. Then had come the pivotal moment: Best, growing steadily more frustrated at the strong challenges he was being subjected to, lashed out at the Sarajevo goalkeeper. It wasn't seen by the referee, but had prompted the Sarajevo players to try and seek their own retribution by targeting him with even more aggression. It culminated in one of their defenders taking a wild swipe at him right under the nose of the referee who, despite mass protests from the Sarajevo players, sent him off. Best clambered back to his feet and, when the resulting free kick wasn't cleared from the penalty area, he was in the right place to volley United two goals clear. Sarajevo's players were furious, this time swarming a linesman who they thought had flagged for a foul before Best had scored.

Dad felt confident enough to allow himself to relax at that stage, but the feeling didn't last. With stoppage time looming, Sarajevo worked some space on their left and a cross was floated deep into the United area. With Stepney having strayed slightly from his line, a looping header from midfielder Salih Delalić dropped over him and into the corner of the goal; 2-1.

In isolation, this was no concern. United were a goal and a man up with time very much on their side. The likelihood of Sarajevo pulling level was remote, but even if they did, United would surely kill them off in extra time. Nevertheless, before the game was restarted, a rumour had begun to sweep across the Stretford End that the away goals rule was in play, meaning another Sarajevo goal would see United's European dream in tatters once again. The November air had quickly been filled with a few desperate whistles from supporters urging the referee to call time.

Away goals was still a relatively new concept in European football at the time; so new, in fact, that it had only been applied in the European Cup for the first time in the previous round. Dad was near certain that the rule only applied in the first round of the competition, but with no way of verifying that he was suddenly gripped by a level of anxiety he'd never before experienced at a football game. The sudden precarious nature of United's lead left him nauseous to the point where he had to crouch down for a brief moment in the hope the feeling passed. It didn't, and when he stood back up he'd been visibly pale. My grandad had ushered him to a marginally less crowded area of the terrace behind them, in case the sudden rush of nerves forced him to splatter the remains of his tea everywhere.

The seconds hung heavy, but United came through the remainder of the match unscathed. The relief Dad had felt at full time had been enormous and his dad had laughed at him as they walked back to the car, unable to comprehend how anyone could possibly become so emotionally invested in a game they were merely watching. The away goals rumour was, in fact, false. Dad had been right: it had been used in the first round but didn't apply beyond that. His panic had been for nothing.

Those five or six minutes had a profound effect on Dad regardless. They were cited on numerous occasions when Chris and I were growing up as a kind of warning. His point, I think, was that you can't truly enjoy and appreciate the moments where your team wins things if you're not made to feel like total shit by them at least once or twice along the way. Without those excruciating, stomach-churning moments, the joy of winning can't be savoured to the full. This resonated more with me as I became older and, in such moments, the image of a young Dad in among the thick of the Stretford End, almost literally sick with worry, would always come to mind.

Victory over Sarajevo put United through to a quarter-final with Górnik Zabrze of Poland, which would take place in February. By then, United had gone out of the FA Cup in a third round replay against Tottenham but had been three points clear at the top of the league table. The home leg came first, where the Polish side held out for an hour before Best drilled a low cross into a defender's shins and the ball ricocheted in for the opener. With a minute to play, 18-year-old Brian Kidd, who had taken the place of the injured Denis Law, doubled United's lead. The return had been played in freezing conditions a week later, on a pitch where the snow had been crushed flat prior to kick-off. Dad had trouble tuning an old radio and only discovered after full time that United had lost 1-0, progressing on aggregate. The goal had come after 70 minutes and the closing stages had seen the Poles heap on enormous pressure. After the Sarajevo experience, it was just as well the radio was dodgy.

The semi-final had pitted United against Real Madrid, who had dashed Matt Busby's hopes of winning the European Cup at the first attempt 11 years earlier. Although they'd beaten Partizan in the final two years earlier, they were no longer the irresistible force of the 1950s. Paco Gento remained but the days of Alfredo Di Stéfano and Ferenc Puskás were over. This, coupled with United's resurgence, meant it was destined to be a finely balanced tie.

Old Trafford hosted the first leg. For a game of this magnitude, Dad had anticipated the Stretford End would be a little more raucous than usual and no place for his 61-year-old father. Instead they positioned themselves in the United Road stand, close to where Dad and his friends used to gather around the railing in the early days.

Real had been unexpectedly cautious, appearing almost content to let United have the ball but stifle their attempts to create. This was undone just once in the first half, when Aston beat his man to the byline on the left and slipped the ball back towards the penalty spot, where Best was in space to lash it high into the goal. My grandad, the cricket lover with no real passion for football, celebrated like the most fanatical of United supporters, surprising Dad by throwing an arm around him when the ball rippled the net. United continued to dominate possession but created little more. It finished 1-0. A victory, but not a commanding one ahead of the return in Spain.

By the second leg, United had blown the league. Having lost to West Brom days after playing Real at Old Trafford, they went into the final game of the season level on points with City, but with an inferior goal average. A win at home to Sunderland was imperative if they had any hope but they lost 2-1 and City were crowned champions after winning away at Newcastle.

The return leg in the Bernabéu came just four days later and there was concern that the disappointment in the league might have some kind of impact. That evening after work, Dad, learning the lesson from the Górnik game, had driven to his parents' house, where he knew there was a functioning radio. He and his dad had tuned in to BBC Radio 2 and waited anxiously around the kitchen table for word from Madrid. The coverage only began at 9.30pm, meaning just the closing stages of the second half were broadcast. When the programme eventually started, the news was bitterly disappointing: Madrid led 3-1 on the night and were on course to reach the final on aggregate. United had been punished for failing to build more than a one-goal lead during the first leg; Dad, who had been nervously pacing the kitchen in the moments before the broadcast went live, pulled out a chair for himself and wearily accepted their fate.

Almost immediately, though, United scored their second of the night. Best had looped a seemingly tame header from the edge of the area towards the six-yard box, where David Sadler had made the most of a fraction of a second's indecision between defender and goalkeeper to flick the ball into the net; 3-3 on aggregate, little more than ten minutes to play.

Dad returned to his feet, the nerves beginning to bite again. For a short while he was left alone as his dad, now familiar with the state his son was reaching, silently exited the room and brought back two whiskey tumblers. Passing Dad one, he gently nudged him back towards the chair and encouraged him to drink. He'd barely taken a sip when Best wriggled his way through a challenge on the right wing and scampered towards the byline, where he cut the ball back towards a free red shirt in the penalty area. Dad would recall vividly how the commentary crackled badly through the broadcast, so much so that he couldn't quite believe what he heard next.

The player in space had swept the ball into the goal, giving United the lead in the tie again. With only ten minutes remaining they were suddenly on the brink of a first European Cup Final.

That fact alone had been almost overwhelming, but the news that the receiver of Best's pass, the man to score what, in that moment, was arguably the single most important goal in the club's entire history, was Bill Foulkes – a Munich survivor and by that stage the oldest member of the team – had added an extra layer of emotion to it all.

After the excitement of the goal had died away, Dad returned to his feet again, nervously lapping the kitchen table for the final ten minutes.

United survived. Their date with destiny confirmed, Foulkes was quickly mobbed by his team-mates as the referee blew the whistle. Charlton was so overcome that he fell to the floor. Busby wept in the changing room.

Dad and my grandad remained in the kitchen into the small hours of the next morning, finishing the last of the whiskey between them. The final would be against Benfica and was to be played at Wembley, and so before turning in for bed, they'd gone through all the calculations. Should he be able to get his hands on a pair of tickets, getting to Wembley and back in a day was feasible. All Dad had to do was somehow get the day off work without anyone noticing.

Pulling a sickie wasn't a viable option. Someone would almost certainly suss him, probably the headteacher, who himself was an ardent United supporter. Dad had just about pushed the thought of attending away until later that week, when he was offered two tickets from a contact at Nantwich Town. Without hesitation, he accepted.

After careful consideration, in the end, he'd decided honesty was the best policy and arranged a meeting with the headteacher where, citing exceptional circumstances, he'd requested the day of the final off. Asked what the exceptional circumstances were, he'd explained he had two tickets for Wembley and wished to go. He'd been reminded that such requests were usually only approved for occasions such as funerals. With a wink and a smile, he'd urged Dad to do what he thought was the right thing. The day off was approved.

In the morning, Dad and my grandad set off, making good time. South of Birmingham ahead of schedule, they stopped off for a toilet break and to throw down a few of the sandwiches my grandmother had prepared for the journey. Returning to the car after their short break, they encountered a problem: the Mini wouldn't start. The key in the ignition was turned several times but the engine failed to splutter into life. By sheer good luck, a passerby spotted them fiddling under the bonnet and offered his help. It quickly transpired that the man had worked in a garage and was able to rectify the problem relatively quickly, giving them detailed step-by-step advice on what to do should it reoccur.

The engine trouble had delayed them. As they approached London, it became clear that arriving in time for kick-off would be touch and go. On the final approach to Wembley, the traffic slowed until eventually grinding to a halt with the old twin towers in sight. Dad hadn't driven to Wembley before. Naively, he'd expected to be able to roll up in the hour before a game started and find a parking space with ease. Just as he was telling his dad to complete the final approach to the stadium on foot while he found somewhere to dump the car, a police officer tasked with dealing with the pre-match gridlock had taken pity on him. Waving them through a small gap between two other vehicles through which only a Mini could have squeezed, a clear line of space opened up on the other side, leading towards one of the car parks at the foot of the towers. Another policeman had been overseeing that car park and appeared inconvenienced that another vehicle had been sent in his direction. He instructed them to park in a space which partially blocked one of the exits, warning them that they must leave as soon as the game was over.

The tension of getting into the ground on time gone, Dad felt quite relaxed as they located their place in the stands, just in time to see Bobby Charlton exchanging club pennants with Mário Coluna, Benfica's captain, in the centre circle.

It was warm. Over 100,000 were inside the stadium. Red-and-white scarves and homemade banners and the occasional Union Jack floated on top of the sea of faces packed into the stands. The majority of the crowd were backing United, which would surely play into their hands.

United, Dad had been surprised to see, wore a kit of all blue. The team was as he'd anticipated, with Kidd – on his 19th birthday – deputising for the injured Law.

Dad had only a few fleeting memories of the first half: Sadler, after his heroics in Madrid, had gone close early on when he almost connected with a lofted Crerand free kick into the box. Eusébio, Benfica's most potent threat, had crashed a shot against the underside of Stepney's crossbar from distance.

By half-time Dad became aware he'd spent much of the game watching Charlton, finding his eyes often wandering towards him in the moments when he didn't have the ball. The sight of him sprawled out on the Bernabéu turf at the end of the second leg against Real Madrid had been a reminder of the enormous toll reaching the final had taken on him. Seeing him finally taking to this stage had brought with it plenty of memories of the painful early years after Munich, where the sight of him on the pitch had given rise to conflicting emotions for Dad. On the one hand, there had been an unmistakable feeling of comfort to witnessing him, an obvious link to the days before the crash, still there and playing such a prominent role in driving the team into a new era. Equally though, those same associations meant that it was, for a long time, tinged with an inescapable sadness.

Charlton wasn't much older than Dad. He'd been barely out of his teens in February 1958 and had witnessed several of his team-mates die at the scene of the Munich crash. While still trying to compute the scale of what had happened, he'd then been left broken by the news that Duncan Edwards, one of his closest friends, had suffered the same fate two weeks later. Knowing that back story, Dad would explain, clouded his ability to fully enjoy Charlton's goals for years. That initial burst of elation he'd get from seeing a ball hit the net would be swiftly followed by the same painful thoughts of 'what if?' when he processed who the scorer was.

Fittingly then, it was Charlton who opened the scoring in the final. Early in the second half, anticipating a cross from Sadler from the left, he darted across the near post and glanced a header into the far corner. Wembley erupted and in that moment it had seemed unfathomable that Benfica could possibly muster a comeback. United, backed by the crowd, would surely blitz them, just as they had in Lisbon two years earlier.

But no. To become European champions, United had one final hurdle to clear. Benfica stayed in the game after

Charlton's opener, surviving a couple of decent chances for United to double their lead. As time ticked on, they grew into the contest and were rewarded with ten minutes to go. A lofted ball into the United box was nodded down by the giant José Torres for Jaime Graça to fire beyond Stepney.

Suddenly it was Benfica in the ascendency. The carnival-like atmosphere that had existed since Charlton's goal had quickly evaporated, replaced by searing tension.

Remembering the words of the policeman before kick-off, it had dawned on Dad that he might, should Benfica force a second in the dying moments, need to make a swift exit to the car, and he'd subconsciously taken his car key out of his pocket. Another attack was launched on the United goal, a simple punt through the middle of the field, which fell perfectly into the path of Eusébio. Two United defenders desperately converged on him from either side, but after his first touch took him into the area, it was clear neither would reach him in time. Fearing the worst, Dad shut his eyes tightly as Eusébio drew back his left boot. The inevitable cheer followed – but it had been loud, *too* loud to be coming from the vastly outnumbered Benfica fans.

He opened his eyes to see Stepney clutching the ball, Eusébio appearing to congratulate him on his save. 'We'll win it now,' my grandad had asserted as the cheers died down. Dad had enjoyed his use of the word 'we'.

The Stepney save lifted spirits and the start of extra time seemed to unburden United. The threat of conceding wasn't gone, but with half an hour to play there would be time to respond if they did. They began on the front foot and were rewarded almost immediately. Stepney boomed a long goal kick downfield, Kidd had got the faintest of flick-ons and it skidded through towards a Benfica defender. There was Best, suddenly, alive to it. As the defender took a tired swing at the ball, he nipped in and nudged it beyond him, finding himself one-on-one with the goalkeeper. Typically unflustered, Best dropped his shoulder and rounded him. The fraction of a second between the touch which saw him beat the goalkeeper and him rolling the ball into the empty goal had felt like an hour. United were ahead again.

Two minutes later, Kidd headed United's third. That goal, the realisation that United were almost there, had brought a man standing on the other side of Dad to tears and my grandad had leaned over to offer him a fresh handkerchief. The emotion was almost unbearable.

Any lingering doubts that the lead might somehow be surrendered were burned away before the first half of extra time was up. Charlton set Kidd away down the United right, then followed his run into the area, veering towards the near post when the cross came in and guiding the ball home. It was over. The remaining minutes were almost irrelevant.

My grandad embraced Dad at full time, then reminded him of the policeman's warning about moving the car immediately after the game had ended. There was, of course, no chance he would be in any kind of rush now. The policeman would surely understand.

Another roar, enough to rival the one at full time, had risen up when Charlton emerged at the top of the Wembley steps to collect the trophy and Dad had stayed for some time afterwards. The floodlights were cut as the team returned to the pitch and were followed by a single spotlight as they paraded the trophy on a lap of honour.

Sure enough, Dad was met with a bollocking by the stern-faced policeman when he returned to his Mini some time later. Two or three of the drivers of cars blocked in had been furious and also chimed in. He didn't care.

Getting away from Wembley had taken a while, but once free of the capital, the journey had appeared to go smoothly until, around 30 miles from home, the Mini had started to splutter, forcing Dad to pull in when steam began to spew from the gaps at the side of the bonnet. Remembering the advice given by the man who had helped them on their journey down, they were eventually able to limp home.

It was over the course of those final miles that Dad had remembered his assembly and settled on the idea of theming it around Bobby Charlton. The finer details of the assembly were forgotten over time, but Dad remembered that he had managed to waffle on for nearly ten minutes – not the expected 15 – about resilience and overcoming setbacks and the satisfaction that can be gleaned from finally realising a long-held ambition. Charlton's ten-year journey from Munich to Wembley was used to illustrate the point his barely awake brain was trying to make.

Chapter 9

Ole at the wheel

UNEXPECTEDLY, GIVEN what had gone before, the final time Dad and I sat down to watch a United game together turned out to be quite a pleasant experience. Three days before Christmas, keeping to the then-recently established routine, I set off for his house an hour before kick-off, stopping briefly at the off-licence on the way to get a four-pack of beers.

When I arrived, I'd been slightly taken aback to see Dad answering the door and it struck me when he did that I couldn't remember the last time I'd seen him up on his feet and not looking on the cusp of dozing off to sleep. I expected his spritelier demeanour to fade away after he'd settled down on the couch and watched the first ten minutes or so of the game, but no. For the first time in a long time, things had felt OK; relatively normal, in fact.

The conversation between us still didn't amount to much, but he showed clear signs that he was at least taking in the match and engaging with it. He'd even reacted to the first goal with a single, sharp, celebratory clap of his hands. I couldn't remember the last time a goal had made him do that.

United were away at Cardiff. The previous weekend, they'd been convincingly beaten by Liverpool at Anfield and, after it had dragged on several weeks longer than it had needed to, José Mourinho was finally shown the door. The club had moved quickly. Having briefed the media that they intended to bring in a caretaker manager, Ole Gunnar Solskjaer was announced on an interim basis. He would remain in place until a permanent successor for Mourinho was found. Or, at least, that was the plan.

The arrival of Solskjaer – or, perhaps more accurately, the departure of Mourinho – had provided an instant lift. Expectations were on the floor as far as the remainder of the season was concerned. A title had never really felt possible, even back in early August, and, by the end of Mourinho even scraping a top-four finish seemed wildly ambitious. Away from their stuttering league form, United had at least navigated the Champions League group stage without too much fuss, only to be rewarded by drawing Paris Saint-Germain in the last 16. Hopes of making it to the quarter-finals were slim. Bringing in Solskjaer, then, was a smart PR move. It didn't matter much that his managerial CV consisted only of winning the Norwegian league with Molde and failing to prevent Cardiff from getting relegated a few years earlier; he was a bona fide club legend. What better way to hoover up the last traces of toxicity left by Mourinho than by replacing him with the guy who prodded home the single most important goal in the club's entire history? Nobody had seemed to complain.

Dad had a fondness for Solskjaer and seemed pleased enough that he'd come back when we briefly discussed it before the Cardiff game, smiling slightly as he muttered something about how he'd always preferred him to Alan Shearer. This, I think, had been an attempt at humour – a nod to a two-week spell in the summer of 1996 when it seemed United were well placed to prise Shearer away from Blackburn Rovers. Dad had become mildly obsessed with the speculation, so much so that each morning had started with the pair of us going downstairs and checking Ceefax for updates before breakfast. When it came through that United were to sign Solskjaer, a name very few from outside of Norway had heard of at the time, Dad had believed it signalled the end of their pursuit of Shearer and was disappointed. Sure enough, Shearer had soon signed for Newcastle and Dad had been in a foul mood for at least a week after the news was confirmed.

Solskjaer showed early in the new season that he was far more than the backup striker most had assumed him to be. Clearly, he wasn't at Shearer's level, but his quick flurry of goals instantly got supporters onside and Dad had quickly grown to love him.

With Solskjaer watching on from the sidelines at Cardiff, United looked vastly improved from the off. Marcus Rashford scored a free kick inside the first five minutes; Ander Herrera doubled the lead soon after with a deflected shot from outside the box. Even though Cardiff had pulled one back through a penalty, United responded instantly with a brilliantly worked Anthony Martial goal to re-establish the two-goal cushion. 'That's lovely football,' Dad remarked as Martial slipped the third into Cardiff's goal. He was right. It was scarcely believable that it was the same group of players who'd looked so lifeless and sapped of creativity in the final weeks under Mourinho.

The second half proved even more comfortable. United controlled the tempo until Jesse Lingard scored a penalty and followed up by adding United's fifth late on. Dad chimed in with another of his 'he's – from Warrington – y'know' comments after Lingard's second – a tiny reminder that, even on a day when nearly all of what he said had been appropriate and in sync with what was happening in the game, things were not as they once were.

Every so often around that time – and there really was no pattern to when they'd occur – Dad would have a 'good day' like this, where things would appear almost normal. My mum would be able to call it within an hour of him waking up: he'd be out of bed relatively quickly and might attempt to instigate a short conversation with her. If it was a *really* good day, he'd go as far as asking if she wanted a cup of tea or take it upon himself to let the dog out in the garden. Small things, but huge given the context of what the rest of life living with him had become.

Acutely aware that that Christmas might be his last, nobody in the family seemed to want to say much about Dad's condition. On the surface, there had been no noticeable deterioration since that awful week in November when we'd been hit with the news about the aphasia and his cancer's spread.

The first round of his last-ditch chemotherapy had been scheduled for the middle of January. That, along with the prospect of further tests to determine the cause of the aphasia, weighed heavy on all of our minds without ever being mentioned.

United were a welcome distraction for me. Their resurgence under Solskjaer continued after Cardiff with consecutive home victories over Huddersfield and Bournemouth. It wasn't just that they were winning again; the football was *good* – genuinely exciting. The safe, pragmatic approach which Mourinho favoured to grind out results on a regular basis had been completely ditched, and United returned to the brand of exciting, swashbuckling play synonymous with the Fergie days. The mood of the entire stadium flipped accordingly. Nige, who, of all in our block, had shown his discontent towards the team and Mourinho the most obviously over the last six months, cut a completely different figure. He smiled and cracked jokes again. He even went easy on the referees. For the first time in a long time, Old Trafford was a happy place and I looked forward to going there.

I'd hoped, after he'd seemed so alert throughout the Cardiff game, that Dad's enthusiasm for watching United might have been reignited. After the Bournemouth game, I knew this wasn't so. I'd been in the press box that day. United had won 4-1 and I'd filed a piece after full time about how Paul Pogba had run the show and looked a player reborn. A couple of hours later, after the press conferences were done and I'd packed away my laptop, I left the press lounge and set off for my car. I'd parked on one of the large car parks reserved for matchday staff, a few hundred yards behind the Stretford End. The five-minute walk over to it took me through the Munich Tunnel beneath the South Stand, and out past the players' entrance. For an hour or two after the game, that area is packed with supporters hoping for autographs and pictures as the players leave the stadium, but by the time I left, the evening was cold and long since dark and the crowds had drifted away.

As I approached the players' entrance, I was aware of a black car reversing slowly towards its doors. It came to a halt about ten yards away, and a serious-faced man talking into a Bluetooth headset quickly got out of the passenger's side. The players' entrance door opened at the precise moment I passed it, and a figure was quickly ushered through it, flanked by a burly looking member of security staff. With our paths set to cross, we both stopped for a split second to allow the other right of way. When we did, our eyes briefly met and I quickly realised who it was: I was face to face with Sir Alex Ferguson.

I'd never been in such close proximity to him before. My days of going to the game in a media capacity had only started after he'd retired so I'd never sat in one of his press conferences. With the exception of one summer afternoon when I was a kid when I'd seen him across the car park at the old training ground at The Cliff and been too scared to approach and ask for an autograph, I'd only ever seen him in the flesh *inside* the ground. Suddenly, though, he was there, immediately in front of me. I was immediately completely flustered. To suddenly be there, standing before someone who doesn't have the slightest clue who you are but has played such an enormous part in shaping so much of your life, is odd.

The interaction was over nearly as soon as it had begun. Earlier that year, Ferguson had undergone emergency surgery after suffering a brain haemorrhage and had not long since started attended games at Old Trafford again after his recovery. Before I'd ever realised I'd done it, I was offering a hand and struggling to utter a few words about how great it was to see him back watching the team. As I spoke, I suddenly wondered if I'd crossed a line and had half expected a firm shove from the security man. Thankfully, it didn't come to that. Ferguson shook my hand and thanked me with a polite smile, then continued towards the waiting car. That was it.

I drew my phone from my pocket as the car pulled away, calling Dad on the house phone. Mum, of course, had answered and seemed reluctant to put him on when I'd asked for him. I insisted. This was important. After a few seconds I heard Dad faintly say hello and began excitedly recounting what had just taken place. I waited for him to respond, but nothing had come back, only the sound of a TV in the background. Eventually, he'd said hello again, and the line had gone dead. Not one of his good days, I thought.

In January, Ethan had turned two on the day before Dad was due at the hospital for the start of his chemo. That evening, we'd invited him and the rest of the grandparents to our house for a birthday tea. Ethan enjoyed himself, plonking himself on the floor in the middle of the room to open his presents in front of everyone. He'd been particularly keen on tractors at that stage, so nearly everything he got had some kind of tractor or farm theme to it.

Dad seemed OK, all things considered. There were moments where he'd been slightly distant, but for the most of it he'd seemed in relatively good spirits. Before he left,

Ethan had sat on his lap and the two of them had shared a slice of chocolate birthday cake, which, before long, had been smeared all over the arm of the chair. The pair of them laughed together as Ethan attempted to stuff tiny fistfuls of cake in his mouth, spilling even more crumbs on the chair as he did. I took a few photographs. It was quite possibly the last happy memory I have of Dad.

The chemo hit him hard, just as the oncologist had warned it would. After returning home, he'd been nauseous almost straight away, never straying far from a plastic bucket. Gradually, the nausea had subsided and he was instead consumed by exhaustion and a need to sleep near constantly. For almost a week, he was bed-bound and needed to be woken at regular intervals to make sure he ate sufficiently. His appetite, however, had dipped sharply, something which can happen after chemo, so for some time his food intake came largely in the form of liquid supplements and high-calorie shakes.

The day after his treatment, when he was still struggling with the incessant waves of sickness, I visited him at home. It had quickly become clear then that he wasn't up to having visitors and Mum and I agreed before I set off for home that it was best to wait until he was over the worst before I returned to see him again.

Over a week passed before Mum called me one Wednesday morning. A makeshift bed had been set up for him in the living room by then, allowing him to conserve the energy which would have otherwise been expended negotiating the stairs – a task which seemed completely beyond him at that moment in time. The room was comfortable for him; a wood-burning stove was regularly fed logs to keep it warm, while the TV in the far corner remained locked on the Sky Sports channels, volume on low, for those moments when he was alert enough.

When I entered the room, Dad was just about awake, eyes heavy-lidded. I reeled off a series of generic questions about how he was and if he was feeling any better than the previous day; he responded with short, barely comprehendible groans. It quickly became apparent he was in no mood to speak but content to listen. I pulled up a chair to his bedside. The chemo had drained him. I saw it as I drew closer to him. His face looked different, suddenly – grey and gaunt. His hair, I noticed, had started to thin, too; small, silvery tufts of it were beginning to collect on the pillow and on his shoulders. I tried to disguise my shock regardless.

I told him about Ethan and what he'd been up to. As I did, a hint of a smile would occasionally break out on his face. When I'd exhausted the updates on his grandson, I dropped a programme into his lap that I'd bought at Old Trafford the night before, where United's unblemished winning streak under Solskjaer had come to an end with a 2-2 draw against Burnley.

Apart from the really big games, I rarely bothered with the programmes, preferring to buy a copy of *Red News* or *United We Stand* on the way in instead. The fanzines gave a more authentic view of the club from a supporter's perspective without ignoring the issues with the Glazers or smothering you in glossy adverts for whatever the club's official red wine or noodle partner was for that particular season. Dad, though, was a stickler for tradition when it came to programmes. Buying one had been firmly part of his matchday routine since he was young and so I'd got him one especially, in the hope that a flick through might help pass some of the time as he recovered.

He summoned enough strength to shuffle himself up into more of a sitting position, lifted the programme towards his face and squinted as he studied the cover. It showed a huddle of United players celebrating a recent goal and he pointed to the player in the centre, Diogo Dalot, and asked who it was, then spent a few moments silently turning the pages. Without saying another word, he'd set it down again, closed his eyes and drifted back to sleep.

The next few days saw steady improvements. Dad slept less. His appetite for food – real food, not liquid replacements – gradually returned. He even began to venture away from his temporary bed in the living room and into the kitchen on a semi-regular basis. My mum had been encouraged that the worst had passed and made tentative arrangements for a family day out to the Lake District at some point in the middle of February. By then, she hoped, he would be up to it. Those plans were quickly forgotten.

A week after I'd visited Dad with the match programme, I had been working in Manchester. Mum had tried ringing twice during the afternoon, but I'd been too busy and only noticed the missed calls after I'd left the office and reached Victoria station to catch a rush-hour train home. She tried calling again when my train approached the platform, but I declined it and typed out a quick message explaining I'd call her back when I got off the train 20 minutes later. If it was anything serious, she'd surely reply to let me know, I thought.

I forgot to call back. The train home had been packed – standing room only – and was delayed somewhere between Eccles and Patricroft. By the time I disembarked with hundreds of other sullen-faced commuters, my focus was solely on getting home in time to see Ethan before he went to bed.

I made it just in time. Dumping my work things by the front door and racing upstairs to read him a bedtime story, I'd barely got a couple of pages in when I'd heard footsteps on the landing outside his room. The door opened and there was Lauren, phone in hand.

'It's your mum,' she'd said – only then did I remember I'd forgotten to call back. 'I'll take over, I think you need to go.'

It *was* serious.

'Your dad's not so good,' Mum told me. 'I think you'd better come down and see him.'

That was all she would say. She wouldn't expand on it when I asked, repeating that she'd explain more when I got there.

When I arrived, the ambulance was already on the way. Dad had been slumped on the couch, shivering. A sheen of sweat covered his forehead. The dog sat at his feet, ears back, head resting on the edge of the couch by his legs.

I went straight over to him and said hello, checking to see if he was responsive. His eyes opened when I spoke, but seemed to look through me, as if focusing on something on the far side of the room. The paramedics arrived, two of them, carrying a large box stuffed full of equipment. Mum began to explain the events of the last couple of days in granular detail. She said how Dad had seemed to be holding up quite well and regaining strength after the chemo but that things had changed very quickly around lunchtime. She'd been in the kitchen and was surprised to see him shuffle through the doorway with a distressed look on his face. He proceeded to tell her that he'd seen a young girl in the living room. The girl had gone missing, he'd said; people were out looking for her, he went on.

Mum had gone cold as he spoke. By then, she had grown used to his bouts of confusion, but this was unmistakably different – something more than mere forgetfulness or the muddling up of names. He was hallucinating. This was new territory.

She had kept it together, guiding him back towards the couch. When seated, she played along for a minute or two in a bid to calm him, insisting the missing girl had been found and that there was no need to worry. He seemed to accept this and relaxed, sinking back into the cushions she'd propped up behind him. She waited with him until his eyes grew heavy and he fell asleep again, hoping the episode had come to an end, knowing all the while that it probably had not.

Around an hour later, he'd awoken with an abrupt scream, instantly clutching at the tops of his legs and intimating he was in pain. Mum tended to him again, noticing the beads of sweat on his brow for the first time. The pain seemed to pass but a quick check with a thermometer confirmed his temperature was running high.

When he'd settled again, she slipped out of the room and tried to make discreet phone calls to Chris and me. Neither of us answered and she convinced herself this wasn't yet serious enough to call 999. Dad was given a couple of paracetamol, which did nothing to bring down his temperature. Another hour passed. By then, the shivering started and he seemed to stop talking altogether, even when asked questions. That was enough. She left the room again to phone for an ambulance.

From there, things moved quickly. Within minutes of the paramedics' arrival, it was decided that Dad needed to be taken to the hospital urgently. The symptoms he was displaying were consistent with sepsis, which appeared to have taken hold with his body weak from the chemo. He was taken into the ambulance, which promptly set off for hospital, blue lights flashing. I followed in my car.

In hospital he was immediately hooked up to intravenous drips and antibiotics and Mum and I were asked to stand in a corridor outside the cubicle he was allocated to while a curtain was pulled across and a doctor and several other medical staff dealt with him. He'd barely seemed conscious.

The sepsis confirmed, a doctor warned us it was serious but reassured us he was at least comfortable.

Dad's improvement was slow. Within two days of being admitted he was moved to a room of his own somewhere on the top floor of the hospital, which had its own washroom and toilet. As the antibiotics began to do their job, he'd started to look better, even if the wild confusion persisted. A different, angry side to him began to surface. On my next visit to his hospital room, he'd become irritated by a clock on the wall opposite his bed, claiming it was the face of a man who was mocking him. He'd started to raise his voice and I'd ended up taking the clock down and leaving it face down on the windowsill.

Later that week, between visiting hours, Dad had woken from a sleep and decided to take himself to the toilet unassisted. He'd been totally alone at this point and, forgetting where he was, the catheter through which he was receiving fluids had been ripped from his arm. Blood had spurted all over his room, leaving the floor looking like that of an abattoir. Fortunately, a nurse had gone to check on him minutes later and raised the alarm as she found him slumped on the toilet, bewildered, trying to work out why his clothes were slowly soaking with blood. Had he been left any longer, he would have bled out.

Dad recovered from the sepsis – if only physically. His face filled out again and lost its post-chemo greyness. He was taken off the drips and antibiotics and moved out of his room and on to a ward, where he was soon able to walk around unaided. Cautious talk about discharging him had begun when he reached the ward, but soon curtailed as it became apparent that the spells of severe confusion which had first surfaced during the early onset of the sepsis showed no signs of clearing. The vivid hallucinations continued and so too did the anger, which had seemed to become more common.

On the afternoon of 12 February I'd visited him in the afternoon, en route to Old Trafford, where United played their eagerly anticipated Champions League game against Paris Saint-Germain. The curtain encircling his bed had been drawn when I arrived and, seeing me walk in, a nurse had pulled me to one side and warned me he'd not been in the best of moods.

I poked my head through the split between the curtain, half hoping as I did that he'd be sleeping. He wasn't, and without hesitation he'd flown into a wild rage at me – first lambasting me about taking away his dog, then about my refusal to allow him to leave and go home. I quickly decided saying nothing was the best policy. Surely, I thought, this was temporary and he would burn himself out. When he didn't, I ducked out of the cubicle to grab a chair, but the tirade continued when I returned.

I positioned my chair close to his bed and he told me to fuck off – a phrase I'd never, ever heard him say before. I tried to hold his hand to calm him down. He swiped it away and told me to fuck off again, louder this time.

The same nurse who had spoken to me earlier ducked inside the curtain and asked if everything was OK. I was aware then that I was shaking and I took the opportunity to step out and speak to her in the corridor while I composed myself. He had been this way all day, she explained, hence why the curtain had been pulled across.

I went back, determined to give it one more try. He bellowed at me to get out. I did. On the walk back through the hospital it dawned on me that, for the first time, my dad might not have known who I was.

I was grateful for the PSG game. On the drive over from the hospital I'd been upset and hadn't given much thought to matters such as the starting XI or how United might try to stifle the threat of Kylian Mbappé. I knew, however, that once inside the ground I'd be OK. The buzz of a big Champions League night at Old Trafford was the perfect thing for drowning out the noise and stresses of the world on the other side of the turnstiles. It was in total contrast to August, when I'd dreaded the thought of returning to Old

Trafford to find someone else in Dad's seat. Only six months on, I found that I wanted to go – *needed* to go. The place served as a temporary escape from seeing him approaching the end of his life.

The game turned out to be a huge disappointment. United hadn't been given a prayer when the draw had been made, but their revival under Solskjaer had given rise to hope that they might – somehow – get the better of PSG, a feeling which had grown stronger when it emerged Neymar would have to sit the game out with injury.

United had looked undaunted by the opposition early on but lost momentum when Jesse Lingard and Anthony Martial were forced off with injuries before half-time. From there, PSG got on top and started to crank up the pressure. It remained goalless until early in the second half, when a corner was volleyed beyond David de Gea by Presnel Kimpembe, who had snuck in at the back post undetected. Minutes later, Mbappé added a second. A first defeat for Solskjaer loomed and the reality of how far off Europe's elite the team were was suddenly plain to see. PSG squandered a couple more chances. Paul Pogba got himself sent off in stoppage time for a dangerous tackle. None of it seemed to matter too much. The tie was dead.

I left on the whistle, thoughts turning back to Dad as I broke free of the crowds.

Chapter 10

Stepping away

DAD'S DISCONNECT with United came gradually, over the course of several years.

He'd first been aware of it in the hour after his Mini had pulled clear of the clogged-up streets surrounding Wembley at the Benfica game, the bollocking from the policeman still ringing in his ears. Out of London, the traffic had thinned with every passing mile and my grandad had quickly dozed off in the passenger seat. Only then – after midnight and somewhere north of Watford – had Dad begun to relax and reflect on what had taken place, not only on that day but in the months and years leading up to it.

Most of all he'd felt what he'd expected to feel: a mix of happiness and relief. For the likes of him, whose devotion to the club predated Munich, watching United finally scale the summit and win a European Cup represented something much, much more than merely seeing his football team crowned the best on the continent. It was the end of a long quest; one which had seemed beyond their reach on more than a few occasions. Knowing he'd seen it through felt good, as though a weight had been lifted.

The other side to it – the side he *hadn't* anticipated – was the peculiar emptiness which had come along with it. The win, he realised, was tinged slightly with an unshakable feeling that the joy of that night and the victory-clinching burst of goals in extra time, had marked the end of an era – not just for his team, but possibly for him, too.

He had seen United win all there was to win. The final objective, the big one, which had hung over all connected with the club for so long, had been met. What else was there left to conquer? Where was there to go from there?

For the first time in a long time, a football season had ended without him willing the summer to pass so a new one would begin. By the time the new season would start, he'd be married. Talk of starting a family would inevitably follow soon after. Other factors such as his job and playing for Nantwich would make him busier than ever in the year ahead. Perhaps, then, all that considered, he had reached a moment where stepping away made sense. The European Cup win had presented him with a natural opportunity to close the chapter.

Before the engine trouble resurfaced and his thoughts turned to his assembly the next morning, Dad pushed these thoughts away. No decisions had to be made at that moment, he told himself. Not after such an emotionally draining day. By the time August rolled around again, the same hunger and excitement for the new season would no doubt be back and he'd likely forget that he'd ever considered turning his back on it at all.

As Dad drove north, United's players left Wembley for the Russell Hotel in central London, where a celebratory banquet was put on to mark their triumph. There was, however, a sombre undertone running throughout the occasion, with memories of Munich inevitable and impossible to escape.

Bobby Charlton, despite his two goals in the final, had been unable to make it to the dinner. The game had been played on a humid evening and, as had been the case after the semi in Madrid, his efforts on the pitch had left him exhausted and severely dehydrated. In his hotel room he had fainted three times before abandoning his attempts to make his way downstairs and join the rest of the team. Though he insisted in his autobiography that dehydration was the reason for his omission, several of his team-mates were unconvinced, Nobby Stiles later suggesting the raw emotion of the night might have been the true explanation for his absence.

Nevertheless, without Charlton, the room had been packed. The players and other staff had been joined by their families. Several former players and, touchingly, the relatives and loved ones of those who had lost their lives at Munich had also been invited. Matt Busby had stood up and sung Louis Armstrong's 'What a Wonderful World' at some point in the early hours, enough to bring many of those in attendance to tears.

Dad's sense that an era had reached its end seemed to be shared by many others in the hotel that night, the players included. 'There was an understanding that something was over, something that had dominated our lives for so long,' Charlton acknowledged in his autobiography. What happened next seemed to confirm this.

August arrived and Dad was aware that the feeling he'd first experienced on the post-Benfica drive home from Wembley still lingered. Partly in the hope he might permanently get rid of it, he took himself to United's first home game, against Everton, played on a day when his own season with Nantwich was yet to begin. United won 2-1 and he enjoyed it enough to convince himself that he wasn't about to imminently lose his love of going to matches.

He vowed to return as soon as possible but, despite his intentions, Dad barely got to any of the other weekend fixtures for the remainder of that season, which – given the way it panned out – was probably no bad thing. Instead, he picked up on the previous season's routine by going with my grandad to the midweek ties in the European Cup.

In October, they'd also been able to attend the second leg of the Intercontinental Cup Final against Argentina's Estudiantes, champions of South America, in a game which would effectively decide the best club side on the planet. United had lost the first leg by a single goal in a bad-tempered contest in Buenos Aires in September, where Stiles had been sent off for dissent. There had been confidence that they would overcome the deficit with the home crowd behind them at Old Trafford but hopes were quickly dashed when Juan Ramón Verén, the father of Juan Sebastián, nodded the opening goal for the visitors inside the opening ten minutes.

Estudiantes adopted a physical approach to the rest of the game, clearly targeting George Best, who was scythed down multiple times. With a minute to go Best snapped, lashing out at José Hugo Medina. The pair traded a couple of blows and were both sent off for their trouble, with some of the crowd pelting Medina with coins as he was escorted from the field.

Almost as soon as the game restarted, Willie Morgan pulled a goal back for United, levelling the score on the night. At the death, it seemed Brian Kidd had scored a second to equalise on aggregate, with most in the ground – Dad and my grandad among them – celebrating for a good few seconds after he had slid in to stab home a flicked-on cross at the back post. Eventually, when it was noticed the Estudiantes players were celebrating, it became apparent the referee had blown up for full time before the cross had come in. The disallowed goal compounded the disappointment of the defeat and frustration in the crowd had seen some of those closer to the pitch hurl more coins in the direction of the visiting players. This, allegedly, at least, had forced them to abandon a lap of honour, though Dad hadn't waited around to see it.

By the time of the Intercontinental Cup game, the sense that United had fallen away after their European Cup success was beginning to build. They'd made something of a habit of being slow starters in the league, but after beating Everton on the opening day they'd embarked on a particularly miserable run – winning only three of their 12 league fixtures before facing the South Americans. It didn't pick up, either. By the turn of the year they'd won only three more, ending 1968 with consecutive defeats at Southampton and Arsenal. By the time they lost a third on the spin at Leeds, they were 16th. The sense of purpose that had sustained the team for so long had gone. This was the reaction.

After the Leeds game, Busby announced he'd be stepping aside at the end of the season – not leaving, but taking up the position of general manager. The announcement had come as a shock, even with United's poor form. The results, Busby insisted, were not a factor in his decision.

United were marginally better for the remainder of the season, eventually climbing to an 11th-place finish in the league. The defence of their European crown came to an end at the hands of AC Milan in the semi-finals, losing 2-0 in the San Siro and only able to respond with a 1-0 win in the return in Manchester. That, though Dad didn't realise it as they walked away after full time, was the final time he saw United play with my grandad.

Wilf McGuinness stepped in as Busby's replacement from the start of the new season. As a player, he'd featured in the same FA Youth Cup-winning sides as the likes of Charlton and Edwards before joining them in the first team, winning the league in 1957 and being capped twice for England. He'd been injured at the time of the fateful trip to Belgrade in 1958 and was forced to call time on his playing career after breaking a leg the following year. From there, he started out on a coaching career which had seen him work with United's reserves and youth sides as well as with England, under Sir Alf Ramsey.

Following on from a man who had been at the helm for so long, though, was always likely to be a challenging assignment for whoever succeeded him. McGuinness's inexperience wouldn't have helped either, but the fact he had to operate in the shadow of Busby, who stayed on in a hugely influential position, added plenty of additional pressure.

McGuinness survived his first full season, guiding United to eighth and a couple of domestic semi-finals. The start to 1970/71 was another poor one, however, with only five league wins by Christmas. A Boxing Day draw with Derby County proved to be McGuinness's last game in charge of the first team. Busby came in to replace him again and was able to steer United to second successive eighth-placed finish before renouncing control again. United appointed Frank O'Farrell, who had guided Leicester to promotion, ahead of the 1971/72 season.

By the time of O'Farrell's first game in charge, Dad had grown used to visiting Old Trafford only once or twice a season – just enough to keep in touch. The days of his life revolving around the home games had long gone by then. Plenty had changed. He and his first wife moved to a larger house. He'd left his first teaching job, moving on to another couple of schools in Warrington, each time seeing him take on more responsibility. In the spring of 1969 he'd also left Nantwich to sign for Warrington Town. Playing for his hometown club over the course of the next few seasons was something he – and my grandad – took great pride in, and seemed to help fill the void left by not going to United as often.

Seeing the alarming rate at which things unravelled after the Benfica final had still been upsetting, but before matters reached their nadir there was enough of a distance there for it not to cut quite as deep as it would had it occurred years earlier.

Amid it all, it was the demise of George Best that had affected Dad the most as he watched from afar. Best had been just 22 at the time he scored what proved to be the decisive goal against Benfica at Wembley, years away from what would, what *should*, have been his prime. If United were to build on their maiden European Cup win, and go on and claim more, it was reasonable to assume that Best would be at the heart of it.

A warning of what was to come came after full time, when Best had celebrated by getting so drunk his next memory was the bus parade through Manchester. The entire night – including leaving Wembley for the celebratory dinner – had been a blank.

Best's celebrity status was already well established before the 1968 final. His role in United's win, however, seemed to propel him to a different level altogether. Though he ended the year by being named Europe's best footballer – following in the footsteps of Bobby Charlton and Denis Law – his reputation for the lifestyle he kept away from the pitch, as a mix of drinking, womanising and a fondness of the party lifestyle was growing. Under McGuinness, several of Best's team-mates had grown frustrated at his lack of professionalism and the way in which the manager appeared reluctant to drop him.

Dad would recall how some United fans had also lost patience with him as his problems became more pronounced and started to hamper his effectiveness for the team. Others were more forgiving, but Dad, who would have killed to be blessed with half of Best's natural footballing ability, had found himself in the other camp, among those who'd begun to resent him. He couldn't fathom how someone so blessed could be so content to wilfully piss it all away. His stance softened as the years went by and he learnt more about the reasons behind it. United – and football in general – simply hadn't been equipped to manage a player of Best's stature and needs at that moment. He was a victim of that.

Dad as a boy, shortly after he and his family moved to the Chat Moss.

Duncan Edwards pictured in 1956. Dad idolised him from the day he first watched him play.

Busby's team line up for a final time in Belgrade in February 1958.

Jimmy Murphy and Bill Foulkes lead United out against Bolton in the 1958 FA Cup Final – Dad's first visit to Wembley.

Dad aged 15 in his school team photo at Leigh Boys' Grammar, 1959.

A young George Best ahead of one of his early United performances. His emergence helped steer Busby's side back to the top.

The immediate aftermath of Bill Foulkes' crucial goal against Real Madrid in 1968. Brian Kidd can scarcely believe it.

Bobby Charlton lifts the European Cup, ten years after Munich. Dad was at Wembley to see United defeat Benfica.

Dad pictured during his teacher training years at Padgate.

Warrington Town 1971/72: Dad (front row, centre) was incredibly proud of playing for his hometown club.

Denis Law (centre) reacts after scoring his back-heel for City against United. That game was Dad's last at Old Trafford for years.

Bryan Robson, a figure synonymous with Dad's rekindled passion for United, lifts the FA Cup in 1983.

Robson scoring in the Barcelona game in 1984, one of Old Trafford's greatest ever nights.

Dad with me as a baby, probably whispering something in my ear about Bryan Robson.

Robson and Eric Cantona after United finally end their wait to be English champions again.

Cantona became the catalyst for my love for United

United return to Manchester after completing the treble.

Dad and I didn't always get on during my teenage years, but our shared love of United helped.

Dad with Ethan. He was desperate to take him to a game at Old Trafford.

'What a player that lad is…' - Wayne Rooney, Dad's last favourite United player, completes his hat-trick on debut.

United lift the European Cup for a third time after beating Chelsea in Moscow. After that night, I only ever wanted to watch United with Dad.

Robin van Persie's volley seals the league title in 2013 – one of the last truly great nights Dad and I shared at Old Trafford.

The chaos following Anthony Martial's goal against Everton in the 2016 FA Cup semi-final.

Old Trafford remembers those lost at Munich before the February 2018 game against Huddersfield.

Marcus Rashford scores what proved to be the final goal Dad ever saw at Old Trafford.

A final glimpse of Best at something close to the peak of his powers coincided with the start of O'Farrell's tenure in the early stages of 1971/72. Inspired by his good form, United were top of the table by the turn of the year, only for things to nosedive spectacularly. Beginning with a 3-0 defeat at West Ham on New Year's Day, United collapsed, losing seven league games on the bounce, torpedoing their title hopes and contributing to another underwhelming eighth-placed finish.

The following season began abysmally with United losing nine times before they recorded their first league win. More defeats followed, with O'Farrell, not helped by the ongoing circus surrounding Best being played out in the background, unable to turn the tide. The axe fell after they were thumped 5-0 by Crystal Palace, a humiliation which, unthinkably, left them in serious threat of relegation, barely five years on from the European Cup win. It was a mess.

Tommy Docherty, who had left his position as Scotland manager the previous month, had been at Selhurst Park to see United's hammering by Palace. After the game he was offered the manager's job by Busby, and was appointed days later. After a winless first month, United beat Wolves in early February and six more victories followed as spring arrived, enough for them to ward off the threat of the drop.

By then, Charlton was weary and told Docherty he wished to retire. Law, plagued with injury trouble, was shipped off to City on a free transfer. Best, it seemed, had quit for good. The heart of the 1968 team was gone.

Just as United were escaping their brush with relegation in the spring of 1973, Dad became a father for the first time as my eldest sister was born. It was, as near enough every first-time parent will tell you, something which changed him overnight. The other parts of his life which he thought had mattered in one way or another could suddenly be viewed with a fresh perspective. This was particularly the case when it came to the dwindling enthusiasm he had for his favourite football team. Naturally, United were forced even further down his list of priorities. Weekends and evenings taken up by being a dad, he didn't play or watch as much football in 1973/74, though he did squeeze a couple of visits in to Old Trafford towards the end of the season, when United were again teetering in a precarious position.

Against the odds, Best had come back for a final time at the start of the campaign, vowing as he did that he had learnt his lesson and could be trusted again. He couldn't. He played a handful of games, scored twice and then, predictably, fell back into his old ways. Docherty lost patience with him when he turned up for the FA Cup third round tie against Plymouth smelling of alcohol, and hit him with a two-week suspension. Before it expired, Best announced his retirement. The last of the Holy Trinity had gone, this time for good.

By then United were in deep trouble. They'd won only five league games in the first half of the season, leaving them in the thick of another survival scrap. Their problems deepened substantially when they went on another long, winless run, ended by Lou Macari scoring the only goal at Sheffield United in early March. Two more defeats followed before a six-game resurgence in early April, where they recorded four wins and drew two. This was ended by a 1-0 loss to at Everton, four days before their penultimate match of the season: a Manchester derby at Old Trafford.

Dad, even as life gradually got in the way, would always try to make the derbies. The rivalry, at least according to him, hadn't been as fiercely tribal then as it would become in later years. In the 1950s, when he'd started going to Old Trafford, it wasn't uncommon for some United fans to go to Maine Road and watch City when United were playing out of town. Dad had never done this, but, after his sisters had both married City-supporting husbands, he would often go with them to watch the derbies at Maine Road without experiencing any trouble.

On that cloudless, late-April afternoon, Dad took up a position in the Stretford End paddock knowing it was imperative that United won to keep alive their survival chances. His memories of the game itself were limited to the final minutes when, for the first time in years, he'd been gripped by that old, familiar sense of nervousness which had once been common during his earlier visits to Old Trafford: a sense of impending doom.

Denis Law was back at Old Trafford for the first time, leading the line for City. In the second half, as City attacked the Scoreboard End at the far end of the pitch, Dad had struggled to distinguish between Law and Franny Lee, who joined him in City's attack. Law was a couple of inches taller, but both men had fair hair which had made it difficult for him to tell them apart from a distance.

Then it happened. One of the fair-haired City forwards picked the ball up on the edge of the United area, his back to goal. Shifting the ball on to his right foot as he turned, he worked an angle for an effort on goal. The ball had taken a slight bobble just before he struck it, causing him to skew the shot. On another day it might have trickled harmlessly wide, but instead fell kindly to the other City forward, who had drifted into an area of space. Checking his run, he improvised, turning and instinctively back heeling the ball. Stepney in the United goal was unable to react in time.

The Stretford End had fallen silent as it crossed the line, paralysed as the gravity of what the goal likely meant registered. Initially, Dad had thought – or *hoped* – it had been Lee who had applied the finishing touch. As a crowd of other City players converged on the goalscorer, it became clear that it was, in fact, Law. Even from a distance, he'd looked wrought with guilt at what he'd just done.

Hundreds – possibly thousands – of supporters had spilled on to the pitch in an unsuccessful attempt to get the game called off. After order had been restored, Law had been substituted almost immediately, the back-heel proving to be his final act in league football. Most, in spite of what had just unfolded, applauded him as he made his way down the old tunnel.

United were down. Condemned to the drop, as some would still have you believe, by one of their greatest-ever players. The truth of the matter, as Dad would very quickly point out to anyone incorrectly stating otherwise, was that Law's goal didn't actually mean anything. A win for Birmingham meant that United's defeat to City was irrelevant. They would have been relegated regardless.

Dad realised when he reached the car that he had no recollection of full time or leaving the stadium whatsoever. He arrived home in time to settle his daughter down in her cot for the night. Years would pass before he returned to Old Trafford.

Chapter 11

How are United getting on?

WEEKS BEFORE the first leg against Paris Saint-Germain, I'd allowed myself to get so swept up in the giddy excitement surrounding United's Solskjaer-led revival that I'd emailed my boss and requested a couple of days off work around the second leg. This had been approved. My plan had initially been to actually go over there, to Paris, though this wasn't something that ever got far enough down the line to discuss with Lauren to see if that was OK. A mate could get tickets for the game and told me one was mine if I wanted it; all I had to do was get myself over there. I'd tentatively looked at travel options but, before I could commit, things had started to escalate with Dad at an alarming pace. The idea of leaving the country, even for 48 hours, had seemed unwise. I wouldn't be going to Paris after all.

After the first leg, it seemed no bad thing. Not only had PSG put themselves in firm control of the tie, United had also picked up injuries and would be without Paul Pogba for the return after his red card. Any faint hopes of salvaging the tie against Kylian Mbappé et al. would rest on a threadbare side.

And so, instead of catching an early flight to Paris – passing the hours before kick-off by sinking a few beers in a pavement café in the shadow of the Eiffel Tower or with a leisurely stroll down the Champs-Élysées – I'd spent most of the day of the second leg in the marginally less-glamorous surroundings of a local soft play centre with Ethan, who was now brave enough to take on the big slide by himself. Evening came. I fed him, and got him through the bath and down to bed by seven, leaving me enough time to call Mum for the latest updates on Dad before kick-off. Satisfied there were no major developments, I settled down in front of the TV for the game, never really considering the fact that United might actually end up going through.

Early on, though, United, wearing their light pink away shirts, had scored; Romelu Lukaku seized on a wayward pass, rounded Gianluigi Buffon and slipped the ball into the empty goal. A pleasant surprise, but something which surely would end up being a mere consolation by the end of the night.

Sure enough, PSG equalised within ten minutes. Mbappé flashed a low cross along the line of the six-yard box and there was the Juan Bernat to prod home at the back post. The two-goal aggregate lead had been restored. Ah well, I thought.

Smelling blood, PSG were on top, looking to put the tie out of United's reach with another goal or two. Ángel Di María was at the heart of much of it and went close with a shot from distance. He'd been the target of plenty of grief from the crowd on his return to Old Trafford in the first leg after his underwhelming season at United under Louis van Gaal a few years earlier. A beer bottle had been hurled in his direction at some stage and he'd responded by picking it up and pretending to take a swig from it.

United dug in. Then, unexpectedly, they scored a second. Marcus Rashford picked the ball up centrally, 30 yards from goal and probably too far out for a shot. PSG's defenders, however, didn't seem in any great rush to close him down, so he'd let fly anyway. The ball had dipped horribly, right in front of Buffon, which caused him to spill it. Lukaku instinctively followed in and was there to mop up for his second of the night. Suddenly – ridiculously – United's patched-up side were only one goal away from winning the tie. For the first time, I wondered if they actually might.

Again, I tried to be realistic. Barely half an hour had passed. The likelihood was still that PSG would be too strong in the hour that remained. There was no sense in getting carried away, not yet.

The first half ended. PSG came out of the traps quickly at the start of the second, missing a flurry of chances. Di María looked like he'd scored, only for United to be spared by a tight offside call. Miraculously, the tie remained in the balance.

PSG continued to create. Into the last ten minutes, Mbappé was slipped through one-on-one against David de Gea then lost his footing at the crucial moment, allowing Chris Smalling to nip in and get a toe to the ball. Bernat's follow-up shot from a tight angle struck the post.

The stadium was tense. You could feel it, even through the TV. PSG, a year on from somehow surrendering an unassailable lead against Barcelona in the Camp Nou, were a goal away from another scarcely believable, sooner-than-anticipated Champions League elimination. Nerves I had never expected to feel at kick-off began to jangle.

On the brink of added-on time, United, having ridden their luck, seemed to be encouraged by the growing apprehension among the home crowd. Forward they went in search of a crucial goal but they struggled to get in behind the PSG back line. In the end it came to Diogo Dalot. With a hint of desperation, he unleashed a shot from distance, only for the ball to ricochet off one of the three PSG players who had moved to close him down, looping up and out for a corner.

I stood up, nerves now fully in control. A set piece, I thought, would probably be the best chance of nabbing the goal.

But the corner was never taken. Dalot's effort had flicked off Presnel Kimpembe's arm as he turned his back. The defender had been just inside the area. Even though replays showed all of this clearly, I'd dismissed the idea that it could ever be given as a penalty. The ball, surely, had been travelling at such a speed when it hit Kimpembe that it would have been insanely harsh – even by the often questionable standards of continental referees. Happily, I was wrong.

The referee asked for the corner not to be taken and began jogging away to check the pitchside monitor at the request of the video assistant referee. Subconsciously, I dropped to my knees when he did this. After watching the replays for what seemed like three or four days, the referee eventually turned back to the pitch, signalling it was indeed a United penalty.

In disbelief, I'd made some kind of loud, long, primitive grunting noise. That, inexplicably, was how the sudden surge of adrenaline coursing through me had manifested itself. I can't actually remember doing it, but know that I did because I was told as much by Lauren, who had immediately come flying into the room with a stern reminder that we had a small child lying fast asleep in the room directly above. Waking him up usually meant another two or three hours spent trying to get him back to sleep.

Glancing at the TV, Lauren quickly understood what was going on and found it amusing that – pathetically – her husband was now so consumed by anxiety that he was sprawled out on the floor, face down, waiting for the penalty to be taken.

Rashford placed the ball on the spot. PSG's players bickered with the referee and did their utmost to delay it, knowingly ratcheting the pressure up on Rashford as he waited.

Finally, after what had seemed like an eternity, he strode forward, striking the ball with his right foot. Buffon had guessed the direction correctly and for a nanosecond looked like getting a glove to it. He did not. The pace on the ball carried it beyond him. The net rippled; 3-1 United. For the second time, I forgot all about my sleeping child.

The time taken for the penalty to be awarded meant that there were still several agonising minutes to be tagged on after the goal. PSG pinned United back for the duration, desperately hurling everything they had at them in a bid to reclaim the lead they'd somehow managed to bungle.

Finally, the full-time whistle came. United, somehow, had done it. Pink shirts streamed away towards the raucous away end in the far corner of the ground. The cameras cut to a stunned Di María.

At home, I collapsed back on to the sofa, the thudding in my chest slowing. That's when instinct had taken over.

So wrapped up in what had just taken place, I did what for years had always been part of the ritual when I'd watched a game alone: I picked up my phone, pulled up the favourites list in my contacts and scrolled down, to 'Dad'; I wanted nothing more than to speak to him, to share the enjoyment with him.

But no. Only when my thumb hovered over his name did the reality come sweeping in again. Suddenly, uncontrollably, I began to sob. Lauren, understanding my reaction immediately, silently put a hand on my shoulder.

The days of me calling Dad for a post-match chat were very definitely over now. That would never happen again.

After weeks in hospital, Dad was eventually allowed to go back home. Following his move to the ward, he'd settled and the furious outbursts which had been commonplace throughout early February had slowly diminished. A month on, I'd find him pleasant on most of my visits, calm enough that we'd be able to share short, almost lucid half conversations about trivial things such as what he'd had for dinner or who else had been to see him that day. What he told me wasn't always true, but at least we were able to talk a bit. That felt significant, as did the fact that, for most of the time, he appeared to know who I was again.

Dad's left leg had begun to swell, making walking around the ward difficult. It was suspected that the cancer had damaged the lymph nodes, causing the tissue in his leg to fill with fluid. He was given morphine three times a day to take the edge off the pain. There was an unspoken acceptance now that the blast of chemo he'd had in January hadn't worked. The cancer had likely raged on and without anyone needing to confirm it, he had moved into the realms of palliative care.

Throughout all of his stay in hospital, Dad was consistent in expressing his eagerness to return home. Cautious talk of a discharge first surfaced in early March, after he'd been in for a month. I wasn't convinced he was ready to come home. Though the anger had gone, he was still susceptible to the wild hallucinations he had first had on the day he was admitted; there would be something every time I went to see him which, even on the better visits, planted enough uncertainty in my mind about the prospect of him returning home, where nearly all the responsibility for his welfare would suddenly be lumped on to Mum's shoulders.

Around the time that talk of him returning home begun, Mum was told that Dad had vascular dementia. When it had become apparent that the hallucinations he was experiencing weren't sepsis-related and those treating him became aware of the earlier GP appointment where aphasia had been discussed, Dad underwent further tests and was sent for MRI scans of his brain. A few days later, a doctor had pulled Mum into a quiet room opposite Dad's ward and told her about the vascular dementia. Stress levels had been running high on that particular afternoon, so she was never really certain if it counted as a formal diagnosis. In some ways, given the rate at which things appeared to be moving with his cancer, giving whatever it was a name hadn't seemed quite as important as it once had.

I'd already read up on vascular dementia months earlier, as Dad's decline became more obvious. I knew other family members had lived with it, too. When it came to the symptoms – difficulty with understanding, mood swings, feelings of confusion, problems with memory and speech – he ticked all the boxes, so the news had come as no real shock.

As talk of a potential discharge gathered pace, Mum made it known that she shared my concerns. She'd been spooked by a conversation with an occupational therapist, who had bluntly warned her of the challenges she'd face if he did come home. Meetings were held and she was assured that, with the right care package in place to support his varying needs, it would be manageable. He had, after all, recovered from the sepsis, she was frequently reminded.

Preparations for Dad's discharge began in mid-March. A care package was put together stating that carers would visit Dad on a daily basis to help him get washed and dressed. This had reassured Mum.

Away from the hospital, the house was readied. The bed was again set up downstairs, as it had been after the chemo in January. After being told that photographs of loved ones are helpful for those living with dementia, Mum had angled a few framed family pictures towards his bed from a nearby windowsill and neatly piled a selection of tattered scrapbooks filled with old holiday photos from when Chris and I were small on a makeshift bedside table.

Then had come the other changes, the things that we hadn't really had to consider before. In the state he was in, the house he had left was no longer safe for Dad to live in. An assessment was done by the discharge team. Handrails needed to be mounted on the walls next to all internal doors.

Cooking knives and screwdrivers and other sharp objects were removed from their usual drawers and locked away. Several large pieces of furniture had to be fixed to the walls. The keys for the front door and the cupboard which housed the electrics had to be kept in a safe place, away from his reach. It had reminded me of a year earlier, when Lauren and I spent an entire weekend toddler-proofing our house when Ethan begun to take his first steps.

Dad had looked unexpectedly normal on the Tuesday afternoon he came home. After weeks of seeing him in nothing but hospital gowns and loose-fitting white T-shirts, he'd been wearing one of his checked shirts when I went to see him that same evening. He was calm and smiled as I entered the living room, back sitting in his chair with the TV on. It was almost as if everything that had taken place since his chemo had been nothing more than an eerily vivid *Wizard of Oz*-type dream.

After a turbulent few weeks, I mistakenly believed that things were beginning to settle.

The next morning, the illusion was shattered. Queuing for an early morning train go Manchester Victoria, Mum had called my phone. It transpired that the calm of the previous evening hadn't lasted long. Dad had gone to bed around 11, dropping off to sleep after being given his dose of morphine. Mum had taken herself to bed upstairs afterwards but remained awake for some time, listening. Around three, there'd been a loud thud and she'd flown downstairs, flicking the light on to find Dad slumped on the floor by his bed, a dazed expression on his face. He'd taken an age to get back into bed, preferring, when on his feet, to shuffle through the house for a few hours instead, seemingly oblivious to the pain in his swollen leg.

'I'm not sure if I can cope with this,' Mum had admitted. It was a sign of what was to come.

Generally, throughout the daytimes Dad was placid in those first few days back. At night, though, things changed. He continued to roam the house. On the third night, he'd tried to move an empty cabinet and inadvertently pulled it over, shattering the glass panes in both of its doors; the following night he'd found a golf umbrella and inexplicably begun to rap the ceiling with its pointed end.

We were told by one of the carers that this was known as 'sundowning', where a person living with dementia might display changes in their behaviour as the end of the day approaches. They can become agitated or confused and this may last well into the night.

Before a week had passed, Mum was certain she couldn't put up with it. The nights were becoming unbearable and she wasn't able to sleep. On top of that, Dad's temper was beginning to resurface again – particularly when I visited. As he'd done in the hospital, he'd begun to tell me to fuck off again, accusing me of somehow contributing to his plight. More upsettingly, he had started to use my actual name when he did this, leaving me in no doubt that his anger was meant *for me* – not the stranger he'd seemed to mistake me for in the ward on the afternoon of the PSG game. That was especially difficult to take.

Things became worse. The hallucinations increased and seemed to last longer. A regularly occurring one would see him lower himself on to all fours and attempt to pick up invisible objects from the floor. He began to clash with his carer, lashing out at him on at least three separate occasions when he attempted to wash him.

Most of the time, he still recognised my mum, but increasingly there were occasions where it seemed he didn't. This, more than anything, had frightened her.

Ten days after he came home, phone calls were made. A social worker visited, then a doctor. The doctor was particularly concerned about Dad's leg and so contacted a consultant, who arranged to visit in the afternoon as a matter of urgency. I had been at the house when the consultant arrived, a tall man, who spoke with an accent which might have been from Northern Ireland but I couldn't quite place. I answered the door and took him through to the living room. Dad was sitting in his chair, Mum perched on one of its arms as she held his hand. After introducing himself, the consultant had asked Dad what was troubling him. He'd slowly lifted his head, scanned the room and pointed a finger at me.

'Him,' he snapped. 'He's the problem, he's brought me nothing but trouble.' My stomach churned. Aware my presence would likely trigger another outburst, I left the room and pulled out a stool for myself in the kitchen, sitting there quietly as the consultant set about examining Dad, who continued to rant about me. I didn't cry – Bryan Robson wouldn't cry – but felt that heavy ache inside me that told me I was close. I knew it was the dementia talking – not him. The words Dad was saying, the anger he displayed towards me, it didn't really *mean* anything. And yet, as much as I told myself this, I felt no better.

Half an hour passed, maybe more. In the living room I could hear the consultant speaking with Mum, who was tearful. He was clear: Dad urgently needed to be readmitted to hospital. The swelling in his leg was almost certainly related to the cancer's spread but needed to be reassessed.

The conversation ended and I walked the consultant back towards the front door. He'd relayed the gist of what he'd spoken about with Mum.

Chris and my sisters were informed that Dad needed to go back to hospital. All of them came back to the house later in the afternoon to see him. After darkness had fallen, an ambulance pulled up at the front. For a final time, it took him away.

Understandably, given all that had happened, I didn't pay much attention to United for some weeks after Paris. That isn't to say I stopped going, because I didn't. Without fail, I still attended all the home games and watched the rest on TV. I'd been holding out hope that, as had been the case only a few weeks before, the football might provide me with a bit of escapism from the grimness of Dad's worsening condition. The truth, though, was that it no longer did. A strange numbness had started to set in and all the emotion I'd usually release during games had gone – already spent somewhere else. I couldn't get exasperated with Ashley Young failing to beat the first man from a corner. Mike Dean would flash a needless yellow at someone and I'd feel nothing. Even the goals – the gleeful moments that make you come back – didn't elicit the familiar rush. I was *watching* football, but in the same way as someone who can see a game on the TV in a living room across the street.

Perhaps because of this, my memories of United's matches in that spell are almost non-existent. The season had begun to go wayward after PSG, just as Dad spent that hellish final ten days at home. I vaguely remember them losing away at Arsenal in their very next game, a result which might have been explained by the gargantuan effort needed to get the result in France. After that they'd blown their best chance of a trophy by losing an FA Cup tie away to Wolves.

That hadn't been enough to derail Solskjaer's hopes of getting the manager's gig on a permanent basis, which he did at the end of March.

With Dad's anger towards me lingering in my mind from the day he was sent back to hospital, I left it nearly a week before going to see him again. Warrington Hospital, where he'd been originally, had been at full capacity when he was readmitted, so the ambulance had instead taken him into Merseyside, and to Whiston Hospital.

He'd been allocated to a ward on the third floor, his bed furthest from the door, next to a large floor-to-ceiling window. On the early April afternoon I'd visited him, the sky was clear and bright early spring sunshine had been flooding into the ward. Dad hadn't long since had one of his doses of morphine, and had seemed sleepy and in no mood to speak when I arrived. Realising this, I wandered over to the window and looked out. The Liverpool skyline was clearly visible. To the right of the city centre, on top of a slight hill, was Anfield. I turned to Dad and pointed this out to him, but his eyes were closed and I'd assumed he was sleeping. A matter of seconds later, though, his eyes remaining closed, he'd mumbled, 'Tell them to pull the curtains across.'

Dad's sundowning continued at Whiston. Concerned about the impact this was having on other patients on the ward, he was moved to his own private room at the end of a corridor, which came with his own self-contained washroom. He'd be able to stay in there without disrupting anyone else. In those surroundings, he'd mellowed and all traces of the aggression had completely disappeared.

My visits to him in this room quickly fell into the same pattern. Usually, he'd be asleep when I arrived, but would gradually stir. His speech would be garbled when he did and I'd spend some time trying to make sense of it. When the words became legible, it would transpire that he was firmly in the grips of one of his hallucinations. Being on a boat continued to be a recurring theme. On other occasions he'd be speaking with his mum and dad – both dead for over 20 years – or about how the man across the road had sold his house. I learnt that if I said nothing and listened, nodding along as he spoke, the hallucination would eventually end and he'd sit in silence for a while when it did.

Then, magically, the vacant look in his eyes would disappear and he'd turn and look directly at me. The fog of confusion which shrouded his brain would lift and there it was, a flicker of the old Dad. And when that happened, the same question would always follow:

'How are United getting on?'

Chapter 12

Hiatus

FOR A long time, the thing that didn't quite stack up as far as I was concerned was why Dad ever decided to go back. By his mid-30s, he was out. After spending a large portion of his life watching and obsessing over United, it had seemed to anyone who knew him at that stage that he'd completely kicked the habit. Following the City game – that miserable, blue-skied spring afternoon of Denis Law's back-heel and the numbness of relegation – he hadn't set foot inside Old Trafford for the best part of a decade; over eight years, to be precise.

A mix of fatherhood, work commitments and that growing feeling that things weren't quite the same after the European Cup win, that something was lost, had all played a part. Without ever making any conscious decision to stay away, a long hiatus had begun.

To my way of thinking, not going to a single game for such a length of time must have made it a damn sight easier to sever the link entirely. After so long, you must reach a point where you're beyond the temptation to go back, free to spend your weekends without being emotionally shackled to a football team, not remotely arsed about how they're getting on at Norwich or Sunderland or wherever they happen to be playing.

But no. Despite his affection for United diminishing to a mere flicker, crucially it was never totally extinguished. Even through the lengthy period away, he always had it in his mind that he'd return at some stage. When, exactly, he had no idea, but as he watched on from afar, he was certain that he'd know when the time was right.

He'd been tempted to go several times in that first season after relegation. By all accounts 1974/75 was a good season to be a match-going United supporter. Though 1973/74 had proved the club weren't too big to be relegated, it was clear relatively early on that they were too big to stay down for very long.

Relegation had seemed to cleanse United of some of the negativity that had swirled about the place for much of the 1970s. Tommy Docherty stayed on as manager, clearing some of the deadwood from the squad he'd inherited and blooding a few exciting youngsters. No longer constrained by the need for unimaginative, survival football, he insisted his team played on the front foot, bringing back the exciting attacking brand of football synonymous with the club's illustrious, not-too-distant past. They started the league season fantastically, unbeaten in their opening nine games, winning seven. As winning became the norm again, they were well-backed home and away; at Old Trafford, the gate averaged a shade under 50,000 for the season. On the road, fans had travelled in huge numbers, packing into every away end.

United never really looked like botching their attempt at getting back into the top flight at the first time of asking. In the end they'd secured promotion less than a year after the the afternoon they were condemned to the drop, a 1-0 win over Southampton down at The Dell, courtesy of a goal from Lou Macari, doing the job.

The sense that United were on the right path under Docherty had grown stronger over the course of the 1975/76 season, when they marked their top-flight return by finishing third. It had ended on a sour note, however, when they fell to a shock defeat to Second Division Southampton in the FA Cup Final. They were able to atone for that defeat by returning to Wembley a year later and – as Docherty had boldly promised they would in the aftermath of the Southampton defeat – winning the cup, beating treble-chasing Liverpool 2-1 thanks to Jimmy Greenhoff's winner. They'd dropped to sixth in the league that season, but that cup success felt significant, a sign that Docherty's young team were on the cusp of even greater things.

Alas, the win over Liverpool proved to be Docherty's last as manager. That summer, he announced via a press conference that he'd left his wife, moving in with the wife of United's physio, Lawrie Brown. A board meeting was held and Docherty was sacked days later. What might have been the dawn of a glorious new era was brought to an abrupt and controversial end.

In came Dave Sexton in Docherty's place, leading United to an underwhelming tenth in the league in 1977/78. There was marginal improvement as they finished a place higher the following season, where they reached another FA Cup Final, losing in dramatic circumstances to Arsenal. Trailing 2-0 with minutes to go, goals from Gordon McQueen and Sammy McIlroy had pulled them level before stoppage time. A minute after the equaliser, however, Arsenal reclaimed the lead when Alan Sunderland got on the end of a deep cross at the back post. Arsenal saw out the remaining seconds to claim victory.

Sexton continued to shape the team to his liking, bringing in Ray Wilkins from Chelsea after they were relegated. For a time it looked to be working as United topped the league in the autumn of 1979 and continued what appeared to be a genuine title charge into the new year only for it to fizzle out in April. Liverpool, still the dominant force in English football, ended up champions again. Still, United's board were encouraged enough to hand Sexton a new three-year deal in the hope he might go one better the following season. He didn't. They finished eighth and Sexton was sacked a year later.

Ascertaining how much attention Dad paid to United in his years away was always difficult. He'd cared enough to watch the big games whenever they were on TV, yet it was clear that not being inside the ground meant his memory and knowledge of the team at that time wasn't as razor sharp as it was for the years when he was present. I know he'd had a soft spot for Docherty and admired his charisma, but the Sexton days had seemed to pass him by almost completely.

Ron Atkinson had left West Bromwich Albion to replace Sexton as United manager in 1981. Tasked with ending the years of drift, one of the first notable things he did came two months into his first season, when he persuaded the United board to pay his old club a British record transfer fee of £1.5m for a midfielder named Bryan Robson. He would prove to be the most iconic United player of the generation, a key figure in Dad's rekindled passion for the club.

The catalyst for Dad going back had been the breakdown of his marriage. The precise details were always a bit hazy and so I never found out too much in terms of how or why it happened, nor did I feel any real desire to ask any questions. The odd minor detail would slip out over the years, but never enough for me to piece together anything close to the full picture.

As far as I can tell, it happened at some point in 1982 and was a mutual decision. The relationship had simply run its course and both accepted the time had arrived to go their separate ways. By then they had two young daughters and the wrench for Dad had been that the break-up meant moving out of the family home away from them. That part, even decades later, I know filled him with a heavy sense of guilt.

After leaving, adjusting had taken Dad a while. Living as a family unit of four to suddenly being thrust into a scenario where he was alone and back under his parents' roof, starting and finishing each day in a cramped box room, had been difficult for him. Left with plenty of thinking time, he blamed himself for not being present enough for his daughters when he'd had the opportunity. Initially, there'd been the commitments he had playing football, which had still swallowed up plenty of his Saturdays when my eldest sister was born. After that, in the years when he'd stopped playing, it had been work. He'd taken a job at a newly opened school near Leigh in 1977 and had quickly been promoted to the position of deputy head. From Monday to Friday, more of his evening time was taken up with work than ever before. On top of that he'd started to lead the school's outdoor pursuits activities, which would often see him taking groups up to the Lake District for entire weekends at a time. He simply hadn't been at home enough at a time when, on reflection, he knew he should have been. That, he would tell me not long before Ethan was born, had been a huge mistake.

The weeks that followed him moving out bled into months. By his own admission, it was one of the lowest periods of his entire life and he was almost certainly grappling with a degree of depression. Although his job had proved a useful diversion during the daytimes, the evenings were a struggle. The company of his parents, who were nothing but sympathetic and supportive to his situation, had been suffocating. Pitching in for an early night would only see his mind race for hours before eventually giving in to sleep. As a coping mechanism, he fell into a strange routine of going out for a nightly drive. In a way he couldn't explain, the quiet of the road at night had seemed to dim the upset and clear his mind in a way nothing else would. He'd excuse himself after finishing tea with his parents and slip out of the door, sometimes leaving for hours on end. More often than not he'd tend to head south of Warrington, out into the sleepier corners of Cheshire, where the country roads were always near-deserted. On other occasions he would drive towards Leigh and Glazebury, where he would find himself driving slowly past the old pub where he had spent the happiest days of his childhood.

Then, one night towards the end of that summer, he felt an inexplicable urge to drive towards Manchester. A short while later, he found himself parking up in one of the quiet streets close by Old Trafford and climbing out of the car.

The new season had yet to start and the place had been eerily still, as football stadiums always are when the matchday hordes have departed. Alone, he spent what might have been an hour walking around, recalling the old days and inspecting what had changed in his years away. The time, he knew then, had come. That yearning to be back there on a matchday that had been absent for so long was finally back.

His need to return wasn't as straightforward as simply wanting to watch United play football again. That, naturally, formed part of it, but it was equally – if not *more* – about wanting to forget the other things going on at that particular time. Entering a football stadium has a mysterious knack of helping you forget the shit that life invariably flings your way. The more invested you are in the game or the team playing it, the easier it is to leave your troubles at the gate and melt away into the crowd for a couple of hours. It was that kind of escapism, I think, that Dad had initially craved.

His decision made, the day arrived: Saturday, 28 August 1982. United vs Birmingham City, the opening game of the 1982/83 season. Dad got himself into the Stretford End early, close to the red fence which segregated the fans from the playing surface. As the ground had filled, it had quickly become boisterous, and Dad, for the first time in his life, had been conscious of the fact he was older than many of those packed into the terrace around him by a few years.

By kick-off the crowd had swayed unpredictably, so much so that keeping his feet rooted to one spot was impossible. He'd forgotten that sensation in his time away. So much of that afternoon was like that, remembering things that happened on matchday that had lain dormant in his mind for nearly a decade. It was akin to listening to a favourite album from your youth. You don't hear or so much as think about it in years and yet, without even trying to remember, listening to the first couple of note summons every lyric and intricate detail back as if you've been listening to it on loop for the past month.

Everything – with the exception of the players' names – had seemed reassuringly familiar that day. He had only vague memories of the game itself, but fondly remembered the explosion of noise which greeted Steve Coppell's opening goal and how he'd wondered to himself in the sea of flailing limbs how he could have gone without it all for so long.

United had cantered to a 3-0 win and from that day forward he was back in, attending nearly every home game throughout the 1982/83 season. Simply knowing there was a match on the horizon had given him something to focus on. Much like the late-night drives he'd become accustomed to taking, it was something he could take off and do all by himself. There would be others around him on the terraces, of course, but there was comfort in losing himself among thousands of strangers. That, particularly in the early weeks of the season, had been a big part of the appeal.

By early 1983, Dad had met my mum, Sue, at work; she'd started teaching English at the same school as him a year after he'd been appointed there and, like him, had been going through a divorce. Her tolerance of his rediscovered need to be at the football every other weekend helped in those early stages.

Under Atkinson, United had improved and finished 1981/82, their first season under him, in third. The football being played was more expansive than it had been while Sexton was manager and things were moving in the right direction, even if they had ended up nine points adrift of league winners Liverpool. Another third-placed finish came the following season – Dad's first since his return – but the gap between them and Liverpool, who finished as champions again, had widened to 12 points.

Disappointment at still being some way off mounting a serious title tilt was softened by another FA Cup triumph. United needed a replay to beat recently relegated Brighton & Hove Albion after the final ended 2-2 after extra time.

Dad had watched it at home with my grandad. Though so much of that season had been simply about rediscovering what it was to be a supporter again after so long away, he'd realised in the final seconds of extra time that he'd very definitely passed back into territory where football – the winning and losing part – mattered again.

With both teams weary, a stray pass had broken to Brighton's Jimmy Case just inside the United half. He quickly lobbed it into space behind United's retreating back line, where Michael Robinson had got there ahead of Kevin Moran and brushed off his attempted tackle. Gordon McQueen had covered Moran and was quickly back to help out, but Robinson checked back on to his right foot and laid a pass to Gordon Smith, scorer of Brighton's opener, who had only Gary Bailey in the United goal to beat.

Dad instinctively closed his eyes – Eusébio vs Stepney all over again – bracing himself for the blow that would surely come. Smith afforded himself a touch to control Robinson's pass, then struck his shot low. Bailey, mercifully, had left his line at precisely the right moment. The ball wedging beneath him, he was able to drop on it. United survived.

Having ridden their luck, United made light work of it second time around. The replay took place at Wembley the following Thursday evening. Twenty-five minutes in, the ball was worked down the United left and teed up for Bryan Robson, in space several yards outside the Brighton box. Striking the ball crisply with his left, it flew into the far corner of the goal. From there, United took control. Norman Whiteside doubled the lead with a header minutes later; on the stroke of half-time, Robson stole in at the back post to bundle home a Frank Stapleton header for his second of the game. The match as good as over, a second-half penalty from Arnold Mühren added the gloss at 4-0.

That cup-winning United side of 1983 was by no means vintage but it was nevertheless one for which Dad held a special affection. A lot of it had boiled down to the fact that was the team he watched as he reconnected. He'd enjoyed witnessing the ease with which Whiteside, who only turned 18 just before the final, had taken to life in the first team. He'd loved the uncompromising, body-on-the-line approach to defending of Moran and McQueen, the elegance and vision of Wilkins in the midfield. But above all, it was Robson. *Nobody* came close to Robson – not that season, not that era. By the Brighton final he was the captain, a player who seemed to single-handedly drag the standard of those around him up a notch or two. He did everything: he scored, tackled, ran until his body was weary and broken and then did his utmost to push on through the pain anyway. Dad adored him. Of everyone he saw play for United – including those who won European Cups and multiple league trophies – only Duncan Edwards ranked higher.

Ten months after beating Brighton, Dad was in the thick of the Stretford End for arguably Robson's finest 90 minutes in a United shirt. Winning the FA Cup had seen United qualify for the European Cup Winners' Cup, where they'd overcome Dukla Prague and then Spartak Varna in the autumn to set up a quarter-final against Barcelona.

United had played relatively well in the first leg over in the Camp Nou but lost 2-0. But back at Old Trafford they'd seemed undaunted, chasing the game from the off. The crowd feeding on this, the atmosphere was electric – the best anyone there to witness it had ever known it to be. Robson had been at the heart of it. Midway through the first half he'd halved the deficit with diving header. After the interval, he'd instinctively followed up Wilkins's shot as it was spilled by the goalkeeper to bring United level on aggregate. The Stretford End had been bouncing by that point, so much so that Dad was sure he could feel the structure of the stand beneath his feet begin to shake.

Barely three minutes later, United scored again. Robson, once more, was involved, slotting a pass to the left wing for Arthur Albiston, whose deep cross was nodded down by Whiteside into the path of Stapleton, who applied the finish. Dad lost his footing in the chaos that followed and wasn't able to clamber back up for what had felt like minutes.

Bewildered by what had unfolded, Barça couldn't respond. Even the great Diego Maradona was almost entirely ineffective as United closed the game out. Supporters had spilled on to the pitch at full time, flocking to Robson and carrying him off the playing surface on their shoulders.

Cruelly, injury denied Robson the chance to play in the semi against Juventus, who beat United 3-2 on aggregate. Disappointing though it was, that night against Barça had given rise to hope that, with Robson in their side, United might be on the cusp of making a serious push for the league title that had eluded them for so long.

It wasn't to be. Another FA Cup win came the following season as they beat Everton 1-0 at Wembley, but in the league United finished fourth, then again the following season. Though Robson continued to be a huge influence on the team when fit, he alone wasn't enough to see them challenge for the league. After a poor start to the 1986/87 season, Atkinson was sacked in early November.

In April 1984, a month after Robson's heroics against Barcelona, my parents had married at a registry office in Warrington. Less than two years later, I was born.

'Here's your little Manchester United player,' had been Mum's first words to Dad in the delivery suite. It didn't quite go to plan in that respect.

Chapter 13

The scarf

THE LAST home game of the season was never a day I particularly looked forward to. Even in the good times, when it was exciting and there was still a league title on the line, simply knowing that it was nearly over, that only 90 minutes of football separated me from a tediously long two-month slog without going to Old Trafford, meant the day was always tinged with a shred of sadness.

Alone and cutting across a large overspill matchday car park off Wharfside Way, that thought had crossed my mind in the hour before United hosted already-relegated Cardiff in the final game of 2018/19. It couldn't have been more different, I'd thought; never had I been more ready for a season to end. I almost relished the thought of full time, of saying my goodbyes to the others and getting back home, to the mundaneness of a few football-less summer weeks.

I had time on my hands before kick-off. Old Trafford was bathed in sunshine and the air was warm so I decided to make the most of it, holding off going inside immediately and walking a lap of the ground at an easy pace, for old times' sake. Save for a few boisterous Cardiff fans on their way into the away end, the atmosphere was subdued, as if nearly everyone else had shared that same sense of wanting it to be over.

United's form plummeted sharply after Paris. What many had hoped was a mere blip after that night in the Parc des Princes had proven not to be. A Champions League quarter-final against Barcelona had seen United comfortably beaten over two legs, while any faint hopes of nabbing that last top-four place in the league quickly disintegrated with a humiliating mauling away at Everton which was followed by a 2-0 defeat at home to City in the derby.

Physically, the players looked fucked. One theory was that the swift transition from the slower style of play demanded by José Mourinho to the higher intensity brand Ole Gunnar Solskjaer had insisted on had been too harsh. The squad hadn't had the right conditioning for such a drastic change and so had burned themselves out with weeks of the season remaining. There might have been some truth to that. It seemed the players, along with a good chunk of the fanbase, badly needed a few weeks off and the fresh start of a new season.

United limping towards the finish post wasn't all though. As their form had fallen off a cliff, a nightmarish scenario had begun to take shape at the top of the table. City had been relentless. For a long while, they'd looked on course to win everything in sight.

Only Tottenham getting the better of them in the Champions League quarter-finals had prevented that, but they were still on course to complete a clean sweep of all major domestic trophies. This, naturally, was difficult to stomach, but made a million times worse by the prospect of what might happen were they to fail. A win for City in their final game of the season away at Brighton would be enough to retain the title. If Brighton so much as scraped a draw, however, that would open the door for Liverpool. Regrettably, they had developed into a disgustingly good side under Jürgen Klopp, reaching a second Champions League Final in succession. A win over Wolves on the final day would, should City falter, see them end their near-three-decade wait to be champions of England.

Understandably, then, given the dead-rubber nature of United's game with Cardiff, plenty in Old Trafford had been distracted by events at Anfield and down on the south coast. Most, I think, were in the same camp as me: hoping that City won on the grounds of it being the lesser of two evils. Nobody would be deriving any sense of satisfaction from them lifting the trophy, of course, but you could just about live with it. The simple fact of the matter – and this isn't intended as the bitter dig it will no doubt seem – is this: everything City have achieved since 2008 is in one way or another linked to the club being bought by Abu Dhabi. The players they sign, the managers they attract, the lucrative sponsorship deals they strike with Etihad Airlines. All of it stems from that. No United fan enjoys watching them dominating the league or playing brilliant football, but there is a small measure of comfort in knowing how all of it has come about. Had their Sheikh bought any other mid-table Premier League team at that particular time – a Wigan or a Middlesbrough – there's a fair chance they'd be up there instead. With Liverpool, though, it wouldn't be like that. Aside from the fierce historical rivalry there, you couldn't really pick fault in how they'd gone about it all. There hadn't been any ludicrously wealthy state benefactor. After years of mediocrity, they'd lifted themselves from their slump by making sensible and often shrewd footballing decisions. They'd appointed a decent manager who'd set about building a squad of good players – often at very reasonable prices. Only when they were on the cusp of challenging did they throw serious money on a couple of missing pieces to their jigsaw. There was more merit in the way they'd done it, which, because of how petty footballing rivalries work, meant seeing them win the league would have been far worse.

I got inside and bought a programme to take Dad later in the week, then wandered across the concourse to the usual spot for a chat with Frank and Nige and the others. Nige was already in full flow, eyes wide as he put forward his arguments for why appointing Solskjaer on a permanent basis had been a mistake and that Mauricio Pochettino would have been a better option. In no mood to get involved, I'd made my way up to my seat on my own, waiting for the teams to emerge at the mouth of the tunnel.

Aside from the usual livelier corners of the ground, the crowd had been largely quiet soon after kick-off, most in the lower tier of the East Stand preoccupied with screening their eyes from the bright sun in order to follow the game properly.

United didn't start too well and it had come as no surprise when Cardiff, woeful all season, had won themselves a penalty. Over on the far side of the pitch to where my seat was, just under the shadow cast by the Stretford End roof, Diogo Dalot had slid in to tackle one of the Cardiff forwards. Though he'd seemed to take the ball, the referee had instantly pointed to the spot and remained unmoved by the following half-arsed protests from United's players. Nathaniel Mendez-Laing had stepped up and tucked the penalty away to put the visitors ahead. The exasperated groans that had punctuated the opening stages grew louder in the moments following the goal, then seemed to die off completely when word filtered through from Brighton: City were losing. Liverpool, already a goal up against Wolves, were on course to be champions. *Shit.* The news swept across the stand, the precious few able to get internet connection on their phones repeatedly asked to confirm that this was indeed the case.

Mercifully, almost as soon as this had started, it was over. City had drawn level within a minute, alleviating some of the panic, and by half-time they'd gone 2-1 up, allowing most inside Old Trafford to refocus on the game taking place in front of them.

United had looked fractionally better for a little while after the interval, yet managed to make matters worse for themselves. A Cardiff throw-in on their right wing had seen Scott McTominay attempt to steal in front of an opponent and get a toe to it. He was held off and it bounced on towards the byline. Paul Pogba had completely switched off at this point, allowing Josh Murphy to dart past him and seize possession inside the box. Suddenly in acres of space, he rolled a pass across the six-yard box to the back post for Mendez-Laing, who tapped home. Cardiff were two up. United, you knew at that point, were done. There would be no response. A season to forget would be given an appropriately underwhelming finale.

By the time full time came around, several large patches of red had already opened up in the stands, the exits down to the concourse already clogging up. The usual chorus of 'see you next season' and the farewell handshakes had long been in full swing around me by then. Remembering last year and Dad's tears as the stadium had emptied after the Watford game, I'd wondered before kick-off how I'd feel at that precise moment. I'd been expecting to feel something – some kind of regret, perhaps – but no.

I hadn't renewed my season ticket. It had taken a few months to mull the decision over in my mind, but by the end of April I was definite it was the right call. That lack of emotion towards the games I'd experienced in the weeks after PSG remained. I was sure that I was no longer enjoying it – going along out of habit or because the money for my ticket had already left my bank account.

It would be easy to have put this down to United being shit. Perhaps, somewhere subliminally, there was an element of truth in that. The more I thought about it though, it was more to do with Dad.

Most football fans, I think, will relate to slowly realising with the passing of time that results are only part of why we allow ourselves to become so pathetically consumed by the sport. Your team winning and losing games matters – of course it does – but so too does who you're spending those matchdays with, the bonds that are forged. While there were definitely times over the course of that season where having a football game to go to helped take my mind off the rawness of his decline, being in a place which held so many memories of him – of *us* – only reminded me of how things could never be what they once were. Doing it all alone had stripped away too much of what made it important.

Oblivious to the final weeks of the season, Dad remained in Whiston Hospital for the best part of a month. In early May, after an oncologist had visited to confirm what we by then knew – that the round of chemo he'd undergone at the start of the year would be his last – arrangements were made for him to move into a care home. To die, was the part left unspoken. Putting an exact timescale on how long Dad had left was vague. There had been no further scans. They, I suppose, are only necessary when there's still hope of treating it. It was therefore impossible to determine where and how quickly the cancer had spread.

We chose a home for him on the south side of Warrington, not far from Cantilever Park, where he'd played for Warrington Town as a young man. They provided palliative care and specialised in supporting residents with dementia, which was imperative. There were three separate floors, each with wide corridors leading down towards various communal seating areas and dining rooms. The top floor, which is where Dad had initially been allocated a room, was where those living with more advanced dementia resided. His room was spacious and comfortable with a window looking out over a large triangular garden area where, on warmer days, some of the residents would sit out on patio furniture and benches with visiting loved ones.

As it was after he returned home following his first spell in hospital, Dad was agitated by the change in surroundings. On the day of my first visit to him, one of the other residents, a tall, bull-necked man who had been a professional rugby league player, had mistakenly believed Dad had taken his room. He'd charged through the door and confronted Dad while he was lying in bed, bellowing and swearing at him until a nurse had intervened and coaxed him away. The incident had shaken Dad and I'd found him being comforted by a member of staff when I arrived. This, from what I could gather, wasn't an isolated incident. Another woman from a room across the corridor also had a habit of wandering into his room on a regular basis, often attempting to climb into his bed with him still lying in it. The woman, who must have only been in her 50s, was unable to speak, responding only with shrill, screeching sounds when trying to communicate. This had added to Dad's anxiety.

Before long, when his needs had been thoroughly assessed, it was decided it was more appropriate for Dad to be moved to the ground floor. So as not to confuse him, he'd been given a room in an identical position to the one he'd had on the top floor. Though every passing week was punctuated with at least a couple of bad days, generally he'd seemed to mellow after the move downstairs. The swelling in his leg, which had left him immobile for long periods during and between his hospital stays, had gone down, allowing him to dodder the short distance down the corridor towards the communal areas. Mum had walked in one day to find him attempting to take part in one of the keep-fit sessions which had been put on for the residents. Though encouraging that he was integrating himself, the vision of him, a former PE teacher, struggling to mirror the most basic of movements from the instructor had brought her to the brink of tears.

More often than not, I went alone when visiting the home. With Dad's mood still unpredictable in the first few weeks he'd been there, I'd reasoned that it probably wasn't wise to take Ethan, who was still only two and a half.

For the vast majority of my visits, Dad had not recognised me when I walked through the door, greeting me with a hint of suspicion on his face, as he would have done had a total stranger entered the room. The damage to Dad's brain caused by the dementia had caused a neurological condition called prosopagnosia. Also known as face blindness, it prevents a person from being able to look at a face and translate what they see into an understanding of who that person is – even if it belongs to a loved one. Though it was markedly better than the aggression he'd displayed towards me only weeks earlier, knowing my own father could no longer identify me by sight had left a hollow feeling. A nurse had suggested wearing items of clothing he associated with me to help him.

My next visit after that had come in the middle of May, after the Cardiff game. I'd opened up the glove box in my car after parking up and pulled out the match scarf which had been left neatly folded inside since the night of the derby the previous month.

In his room, Dad had been slumped in an armchair, staring vacantly at the near-silent TV mounted on the wall opposite his bed. He'd turned his head towards me.

'Hello Dad,' I'd said, but no response came back. I'd pulled up a stool and sat by his chair as he gradually began to utter a few whispered words about needing to finish some decorating in the back room. I'd got up to turn the TV off. 'You can leave it, Brian,' he'd told me, and so I sat back down. Dad continued to speak in barely decipherable sentences until I remembered the scarf, which I'd left on top of a chest of drawers by the door with the programme from the Cardiff game. I reached over for it, draping it over the arm of his chair as subtly as I could. He clocked it immediately, picking it up and studying it in silence for a matter of seconds before setting it back down again and twirling the white tassels at the end between a finger and thumb. Looking up at me again, he spoke.

'Did you go watching them this week, Sime?' he asked.

'Yeah,' I replied, swallowing hard, then handed over the programme to him. He picked it up and clumsily flicked through a few pages.

'What a player, eh?'

'Who?'

'Cantona.'

A long pause followed. 'You can turn that off, Brian,' he said, nodding gently in the direction of the TV. And with that, Dad had gone again.

I'd taken the scarf with me for nearly every visit after that day. I'd also tried to wear a football shirt of some description, making it easier for him to make the connection that it was me who'd come to see him. I hadn't bought a United shirt in years so would often dip into the collection of foreign club shirts I'd accumulated over the years. On one occasion, I'd worn an Athletic Club shirt I'd picked up on a work trip to Bilbao the previous year. Dad had been barely lucid that day but had suddenly taken an interest in the red and white stripes and began to squint his eyes as he tried to study the badge on my chest. I'd explained it belonged to Athletic Club, from Bilbao in Spain.

'Maine Road,' he'd responded in a gruff voice, '3-0.' Only on the drive home did the penny drop: as a kid, he'd watched United beat Athletic in that first season in the European Cup back in 1957. This was one of the fixtures they'd been forced to play at Maine Road due to Old Trafford's lack of floodlights. That had been what he was trying to say.

Summer came. When warm enough, I'd wheel Dad out into the garden area and the two of us would sit under the shade of a parasol on the patio area. Confident that his bouts of anger were now behind him, I'd taken Ethan along with me a couple of times. He'd been pleased to see his grandad again and would insist whenever he came on taking along one of his ever-expanding fleet of toy tractors to show him. Dad had seemed to enjoy his company on the few occasions he visited, though I was rarely convinced he knew who the child in front of him actually was.

The pattern that had first begun in hospital, where, after a few minutes of me arriving, Dad would spontaneously snap out of his faraway state and ask how United were getting on had continued. The conversation that followed that opening question would vary. I'd respond with an update about the current team and, because it was summer, Solskjaer's rumoured transfer targets ahead of next season. Sometimes he'd be able to half-follow it and make reference to Marcus Rashford or Juan Mata or one of the other modern-day players. More often, though, he'd hark back to a bygone era, talking as if it was the present. Usually this would take the form of a general comment about Robbo or Roy Keane and sometimes as far back as Charlton or even Duncan, but he'd occasionally make reference to a specific goal or incident as if it had happened the previous night. The challenge for me would be trying to quickly identify the game that had randomly made its way to the front of his mind so as to prolong the conversation a while longer.

'What about that second goal though?' he'd asked one late July afternoon. 'I thought he'd gone too wide.' I'd racked by brains and found nothing so asked who he'd meant. 'Hughesy,' he'd replied in a mildly indignant tone, irritated that I could have possibly let it slip my mind. He'd been talking bout the European Cup Winners' Cup Final over in Rotterdam in 1991.

There really was no pattern to it. He'd made reference to a Paul Scholes goal in a Champions League group game against Panathinaikos; another time it was Robin van Persie's volley against Aston Villa, then the time Andrei Kanchelskis scored a hat-trick in the derby.

There was rarely much in the way of context beyond it being United, but that didn't matter. Those moments had kept me going back. In a totally selfish way, I had needed them. It was, by then, patently clear Dad wouldn't see the year out. And while so much of him had already gone for good, him talking to me about United for a short while was something to hold on to, something I knew I had to make the most of before that went too. While I was thankful we still had it, it was simultaneously the hardest part. For a matter of seconds – maybe minutes, if lucky – I'd get Dad – the *old* Dad – back. Each time I did I'd hope that everything that had gone before had been some kind of mistake, that it wasn't dementia or the cancer after all and just a temporary phase that he'd finally pulled through.

Then I'd watch as the animation on his face would begin to fade, his eyes would glaze over and, before I knew it, he was gone again. And, as anyone who's ever seen a loved one live with dementia will tell you, no matter how many times you witness that, it destroys you every single time.

Chapter 14

Eric (not Clayton)

I NEVER stood a chance, really. Before I'd so much as drawn my first breath, Dad had decided that when the time eventually came around for my first taste of Old Trafford, I'd be well prepared and sufficiently brainwashed for the occasion to mean something, to stick in my memory.

And so, stupidly early in my life, he'd made it his mission to expose me to a steady stream of all things United. Most of it, I suppose, was probably the kind of stuff you'd expect a football-besotted father to subject their young child to: the buying of replica kits when they'd barely mastered walking; the making sure Father Christmas inexplicably throws in a few unasked-for pieces of club merchandise under the tree each year; teaching them the words to various songs from the terraces as if they're nursery rhymes. That sort of thing, as I now know from my own experience as a father, is par for the course. With Dad, though, it didn't really to stop there.

It occurred to me during his final months, amid the maelstrom of emotions stirred up by those countless *how are United getting on* chats we shared, that, because of him, I couldn't actually remember a time when United hadn't been there. Some of my very earliest memories were coloured by a vague understanding of this thing called 'United', even if the intricacies of the sport they played and what it meant to be a supporter were yet to be discovered.

Just about the first thing I remember in my life is a tiny, snapshot memory from around the time I turned three. We'd been preparing to move house to somewhere nearer to the school where my parents taught. I've no recollection of the old house we lived in, but can remember standing in its small back garden with Dad one spring day when a collared dove had briefly settled on top of a fence next to a tall conifer tree. The bird had puffed out its chest and started making a noise. 'Listen,' Dad had said to me excitedly, pointing towards it, then began chanting along to the bird's three-syllable coo, 'U-niii-ted… U-niii-ted.' Ridiculously, that moment has stayed with me, meaning to this day I can't hear a collared dove without a part of my mind imagining it's a staunch Stretford Ender, willing the team on to a late winner.

By the time I'd turned five, Dad had grown impatient at my apparent lack of interest in it all. He couldn't fathom why, despite his relentless efforts, I was more concerned with playing Ghostbusters or Teenage Mutant Ninja Turtles than paying even the tiniest shred of attention to United. In his head, I think he'd expected that I'd be a regular on matchdays by then. He continued to go to games alone, leaving each match programme by my bedside when he returned home, clinging to a diminishing hope that it might someday pique my curiosity.

In the middle of the 1992/93 season, there had finally come a breakthrough. Eric Cantona, fittingly, was the catalyst, just as he was for just about everything else that followed for United in the years to come.

The timing, I've often thought, was perfect. If Dad had possessed the power to engineer a set of circumstances in which his young son would be enticed into following his team, what happened from November 1992 onwards would have been something extremely close to what he would have drawn up.

I'd only been eight months old when Alex Ferguson had taken the United job. This, therefore, meant that I was too preoccupied with teething and potty training and learning to walk and talk to care too much about the turbulence of his first three and a bit years in charge.

After a 2-1 defeat at home to Crystal Palace in December 1989, Dad was convinced Fergie's time was up, such was the level of grief he was getting from some sections of the crowd. He survived though, and – courtesy of Mark Robins scoring a winner at Nottingham Forest a few weeks later – oversaw the run to the FA Cup Final against Crystal Palace which is widely believed to have kept him in a job.

That final, I think, was the first United game I was actually old enough to be aware of. It finished in a 3-3 draw after extra time, with Mark Hughes scoring twice for United. In the aftermath of one of his goals, Dad had picked me up while celebrating and shouted something about 'Hughesy'. Though confused, I was at least able to make the connection that it was something to do with what was happening on the TV in the corner of the room.

United won the replay thanks to a Lee Martin goal and from there things gathered pace nicely. In the league they rose to sixth in the 1990/91 season, but won the European Cup Winners' Cup against Barcelona in Rotterdam. Youngsters Ryan Giggs and Lee Sharpe began to play an increasingly prominent role with the first team as they won a League Cup a year later. Had they not been shafted by an obscene fixture pile-up in April, they might have clinched their first league title in 25 years that same season.

And then came Eric.

Cantona had helped Leeds pip United to the title in 1991/92, having only arrived in England in the January. After falling out with manager Howard Wilkinson, United were on hand to snap him up in the November of the same year for £1m.

United had made an inauspicious start to the 1992/93 season, struggling for goals. Cantona, though, changed everything. He settled into his new surroundings outrageously quickly, contributing to a sharp upturn in the team's form. Not only did he score regularly, his imagination and creativity helped his new team-mates do the same.

Before long, Dad was eulogising about him. Cantona had initially been moved into a modest detached house owned by the club in Boothstown, just up the East Lancs Road from where we lived. Dad had got wind of this and – in a move which, with hindsight, was quite strange – drove me up to see it one night after I'd finished school.

I was six by then. Though United still wasn't something which mattered to me too much, talk of this Cantona bloke had become unavoidable – if not from Dad then from some of the older boys at school. I discovered he was French, which had fascinated me. I'd been to France on holiday. I knew it was far enough away that you needed to spend a day in the car and then get on a ferry across the sea to get there. I also knew that in France they didn't speak our language. This had helped generate a sense of mystery and intrigue. It was hard to fathom in my six-year-old mind that a man from such a faraway place, who didn't even speak the same language as me, could be living just down the road, playing football for a team my dad saw play every other week.

The seed had grown from there. Dad would come back from games and tell me the score and I'd respond by asking him if he'd seen Cantona. This became a regular thing. In a bid to impress Dad, I'd once cut out a picture from one of the programmes he'd brought me back from Old Trafford, leaving it on the kitchen table so he'd see it when he got home from work that evening. He'd come into my bedroom later, smiling, asking me why I'd cut the picture out. 'Because Cantona's my favourite player,' I'd told him. So as not to crush my growing enthusiasm, he'd paused and softly broken it to me that the man in the cut-out picture was actually Clayton Blackmore.

Just as my interest with Cantona was taking hold, United sealed their first league title since 1967. Dad, having earlier that season been issued with a stern bollocking from my mum for accidentally taping an episode of *Match of the Day* over video footage of me as a baby, bought a pack of blank VHS tapes and recorded everything relating to the title win that appeared on terrestrial TV. Through the grainy footage of those tapes I began to piece it all together. Finally, I knew who Bryan Robson was; I was able to put faces to the names Giggs and Hughes and Peter Schmeichel. Most importantly of all, I was able to distinguish Eric Cantona from Clayton Blackmore.

Video recordings of *Match of the Day* were essential in sparking my passion for United. It was the only means I had of watching the team at that time. The 1993 title win had coincided with the dawn of the new Premier League era, meaning nearly all the big top-flight games were broadcast live only on Sky Sports. Anyone wanting to watch would have to stump up some money for a satellite dish for the privilege. Dad had been outraged by the concept and, for as long as he possibly could, stuck rigidly to a vow not to cave in and get Sky. For this reason, Channel 4's *Football Italia* offering was the only live football shown in our house at weekends.

Keen to nurture my growing interest in United, Dad routinely recorded *Match of the Day* for me every Saturday night from the beginning of the 1993/94 season, winding the tape back in the old, clunky Toshiba VHS player to the point where United's highlights were about to begin.

On Sunday mornings, I was given special permission to go downstairs alone and press the play button. More often than not, Dad would come down with me and we'd watch it together.

Perhaps it was because it was the season of my first game and when I'd started to attend games regularly, but 1993/94 – especially the last few months of it – was a time when the embryonic feelings I'd developed for United intensified and became something more meaningful. The moment of realisation had come when I'd unexpectedly burst into tears when Aston Villa had beaten United in the League Cup Final in late March, the day before I turned eight. Results of football matches, I was suddenly aware, had the ability to make me feel happy or sad. Few things in life were important enough to do that.

Weeks later, United had wrapped up another league title and then put four past Chelsea to win the FA Cup in pissing-down Wembley rain to complete a double. We'd not been able to get tickets for the final. That, I would come to learn, was often the way of it – football supporters, even in the mid-1990s, got a rough deal when it came to ticket allocations for the games they most deserved to be at. Nevertheless, I'd enjoyed simply sitting beside Dad and watching from the couch, vaguely aware of an unexplainable feeling that the achievements of the men wearing red shirts somehow belonged to *us*, too.

'It won't always be like this,' Dad had said after full time, a warning he repeated near enough every time United won anything of note over the next 25 years. 'You're very lucky to be seeing your team winning things.'

The following season seemed to serve as harsh proof of this, as United lost the league on the last day to Blackburn then went down 1-0 to Everton in the FA Cup Final a week later. In the European Cup, they'd been thumped 4-0 by

Barcelona in the Camp Nou – a reminder that, despite their status in England, they were still some way off the pace of other continental clubs.

Cantona, meanwhile, was hit with a lengthy ban for his notorious kung-fu kick on a Crystal Palace supporter during a game at Selhurst Park in January. It hadn't seemed like such a big deal when Dad had explained what had happened the following morning over breakfast, but then I saw it being talked about on the news and a boy in one of the older classes at my school had been sent to the headteacher's office for recreating it on a dinner lady at break time and I realised it probably was quite serious after all.

In Canton'a absence, three more senior players were shown the door: Paul Ince was sold to Inter Milan, Andrei Kanchelskis moved to Everton and Mark Hughes joined Chelsea. Surprisingly, no major signings came in to replace them.

Despite the lingering disappointment of the previous season, I was fully invested. I saved pocket money all summer long to be able to buy myself the disgusting grey away shirt they ended up ditching when it became apparent the players couldn't see one another properly when they wore it. Not content with the shirt alone, I'd pestered Dad to take me to Old Trafford as soon as the school holidays had started so that I could get a name and number printed on the back of it. I knew there was a booth at the side of the club shop that did shirt printing on the spot.

A year earlier, I'd come mightily close to getting Kanchelskis and the number 14 on the reverse of a home shirt. Dad hadn't been keen on the idea from the start. As we approached the front of the queue, he realised the cost of the printing was calculated by the amount of letters and numbers required, meaning Kanchelskis was just about the most expensive option I could have gone for. 'What about

David May?' he'd suggested, keeping his voice low. 'They've just signed him from Blackburn. He's good.' I postponed my shirt printing for another year.

Before the 1995/96 season started, Dad reluctantly agreed to take me. Despite Cantona's suspension I was definite that I wanted his name and number seven and handed over the money. I'd been delighted and put the shirt on immediately. Later that very day, the news had broken that Cantona, angered at speculation that he had breached terms of his ban by playing in a behind-closed-doors friendly against Rochdale, had handed in a transfer request. I'd learnt the news while kicking a ball about with some of the other kids who lived in our street. I'd initially assumed it was a joke but, realising it might not be, hurried inside to check Ceefax with Dad. It was true. I was inconsolable.

Mercifully, Alex Ferguson was able to change Cantona's mind. He stayed put, playing a leading role as United went on to clinch another double. The climax had come as he scored the winner against Liverpool in the FA Cup Final, sparking wild scenes in the United end and in our back room.

That season was possibly my favourite of all. I'd been in that sweet-spot age where football was freshly an obsession, innocent enough for the depressingly relentless commercialisation of the sport to barely register. United were quicker than any other club to realise financial opportunities that were available to them at the dawn of the Premier League era. Old Trafford had a museum and a megastore by the mid-1990s, both of which were open on non-matchdays. The place was rapidly becoming as much a tourist attraction as a stadium and the club's success and soaring popularity had seen the expansion of the North Stand take place as the season went on. While none of this had bothered me, Dad had struggled with the rate at which Manchester United seemed to be evolving into something more than the football club he'd grown up with.

The football had gone some way to making up for it. United played superbly for much of the second half of the season, chipping away at the seemingly unsurmountable lead Newcastle had built up at the top of the table in the autumn. Cantona was at the heart of it, but the way in which a crop of inexperienced homegrown lads – Paul Scholes, Nicky Butt, David Beckham and the Neville brothers – had filled the spaces in the squad vacated by those who'd been moved on had been just as enjoyable to witness, especially for those old enough to remember the days of the Babes. Along with Ryan Giggs, who'd long been a first-team regular by then, United had the foundation of a team that would see them dominate for years to come. Part of the thrill was to wonder where that group might take them.

The only negative to it was that Dad and I had gone into the final weeks knowing we'd be stepping back from it all after summer. My growing love for football meant that I'd already begun playing for a local team on a Sunday morning. This would shift to a Saturday at the start of the 1996/97 season, making it impossible to get over to Old Trafford in time for kick-off after my own game had finished. Dad had understandably wanted to watch me and soon became heavily involved with the coaching side of the team I played for. Our trips to United were therefore limited almost exclusively to European nights for a good few years from then. Having seen United win the league and FA Cup a couple of times each by then, it didn't seem to matter too much. The prospect of winning a second European Cup was becoming the focus for the club. We'd still be there for those games.

When United returned to the Champions League in 1996/97, things had changed. The three-foreigner rule which had contributed to the mauling they'd suffered to Barcelona in the Camp Nou two years earlier had been abolished, meaning they could field their strongest available XI each game.

They were drawn in the same group as Juventus, reigning European champions and a team stuffed full of plenty of names familiar to us thanks to the weekly Serie A offering on Channel 4. At a time when United were developing and still relatively inexperienced in Europe, Juve were the benchmark, the elite level to be strived for.

The opening group game in Turin had seen Juve win 1-0 thanks to an Alen Bokšić goal. United rebounded with consecutive wins against Rapid Vienna at home and then away to Fenerbahçe. With hopes of qualification for the knockout stages raised, they suffered a shock defeat in the return against Fenerbahçe – losing their proud unbeaten home record in Europe in the process. That heaped added pressure on for the already eagerly anticipated home game against Juve.

Dad and I had been in the East Stand for that match, one of few occasions I can recall where I'd been genuinely awestruck by the opposition. Juve weren't especially dominant, but Alessandro Del Piero had been electric, eventually winning and converting the penalty that settled the game.

United made it through to the knockouts with a win in Vienna in their final group fixture, then breezed through a quarter-final with Porto after an emphatic 4-0 win in the first leg. Dad had been childishly excited on the walk back to the car after full time, adamant that United were destined to be European champions again by the end of the season.

The first leg of the semi against Borussia Dortmund, however, saw United lose 1-0 in Germany. Although there was hope they could overturn the deficit in the home leg, Lars Ricken scored the killer away goal after only eight minutes. United were stunned and unable to muster a response. Dortmund progressed to the final.

After winning the league again, Eric Cantona retired that summer, later citing a lack of passion and the club's increasing emphasis on commercialism over football as factors behind his decision. There'd been a feeling all season that his level had dipped and the news hadn't felt like too much of a shock when confirmation arrived. Teddy Sheringham was signed as a replacement but the loss of such a hugely influential figure inevitably led to an underwhelming season in which Arsenal won the Premier League and FA Cup while United finished without a trophy.

Hopes of bettering the previous season's Champions League performance had also died in the quarter-finals, when United went out to an away goal against Monaco. There was, however, a hint of what was to come in the group stages, when United had beaten Juventus 3-2 at home. That night served as evidence that, even with Cantona gone, they were capable of beating the best in Europe on their day.

Nobody, though, could have envisaged what would unfold over the course of the next season.

Chapter 15

Manchester United 3 Brighton 1

TOWARDS THE end, it became a routine. On the weekend days when United were playing and I wasn't in work, I'd drive over to the home in time for kick-off and pull up a chair to the foot of Dad's bed. He'd lie there, completely still, sometimes able to murmur a few barely decodable words but usually near comatose due to the increased morphine doses.

After I had said hello, I would pick up the remote control and turn his TV on, flicking it over to the digital radio channels to find the commentary on 5 Live. The volume on low, I'd sit with him until the game was over, relaying any major developments. Occasionally he'd respond with a grunt or a gentle squeeze of my hand.

After a couple of such visits, I'd wondered to myself what the point in it was. Even before the dementia was factored in, there was a decent chance the drugs he was on had taken Dad somewhere far away, where United vs Crystal Palace or whoever else didn't reach. Even if it did get through, what did it really matter? It wasn't as if he'd be around to see if they'd sneak into a Champions League spot the following May. Again, I was aware that, like the chats we'd shared throughout the summer, this was fuelled partly by my own selfishness. It was something I did to help me cope as much as anything. Then had come a game against Leicester on a

Saturday afternoon in the middle of September where, when I arrived, a nurse had pulled me to one side and explain he'd been having a particularly bad day. When I got in the room, he'd been crying and asking for his mother. Realising he wasn't settling, I'd put on the radio. Within minutes, the faint hum of the commentary had seemed to soothe him.

I did this for a final time on a bright Sunday afternoon in late November. Just before the last international break of the calendar year, United had hosted Brighton. When I'd arrived, the curtains were drawn, the only light coming from a dim table lamp in the far corner of his room. One of the nurses had been at his bedside when I entered, trying but failing to feed him several teaspoonfuls of yoghurt. Seeing me arrive, she'd set the yoghurt down and ushered me back out into the corridor to update me. He'd eaten next to nothing for two days and had needed near constant pain relief, she told me. She assured me nothing was imminent but had followed this by asking when my mum would next be visiting, which had seemed to suggest otherwise.

I'd re-entered the room and sat by Dad, grabbing his hand to shake as I said hello, aware as I held it of how frail it had felt. His half-open eyes had briefly looked over at me, drowsily.

'You want the game on, Dad?' I'd asked, and he'd forced a wheezy, one-syllable noise out in response which I interpreted as being a yes. I turned it on.

The 2019/20 season had begun three months earlier, with United sweeping aside Chelsea 4-0 in their opening fixture. After not renewing my season ticket I'd half expected to feel some kind of regret that day, that the long summer break might have washed away what I'd been feeling back in May. That hadn't been the case at all.

I'd been working up in Newcastle on the morning of the Chelsea game. By kick-off, I was aboard a crowded

TransPennine Express train bound for Manchester Piccadilly, keeping up to speed with the goals via the occasional glance at Twitter. That in itself had felt significant; in years gone by I'd have almost certainly postponed my journey home in such circumstances, finding a pub to watch it before getting a later train. That it hadn't even crossed my mind to do this confirmed that the detachment I'd felt towards the end of the previous season hadn't been a temporary thing.

United had spent big on bringing in Harry Maguire and Aaron Wan-Bissaka in the summer to help bolster their back line. Dan James, who'd nearly joined Leeds from Swansea earlier in the year, had also arrived. Though the trio had performed well enough up to then, as a team the early weeks of the season had felt like a continuation of the last, their form stuttering. The victory over Chelsea had been flattering. That had been followed by a draw at Wolves and a shock 2-1 defeat at home by Crystal Palace. They ended August with another draw, away at Southampton.

Concern was growing already. United hadn't won a single game away from home since Paris Saint-Germain in March.

Despite all this, I felt nothing. The need to be at the matches hadn't returned; there was no real disappointment when United played shit and dropped points. I'd still watch those games that didn't fall on a weekend day on TV, but more out of habit than any burning desire to do so.

I knew that, in a way someone who understands psychology far better than I do could probably explain, the disconnect was related to Dad. Those *how are United getting on* chats I'd craved so much had dried up by late August. Physically, it was evident by September and the day of the Leicester game that the cancer was progressing quickly. The pain was the main giveaway, but there were obvious signs in his appearance. His face, which had filled out over the summer after his chemo had ended, had looked gaunt again, the skin sallowed and hanging loose below his jaw when he was propped up in bed. His leg had ballooned again, worse than it had been before. As a result, his mobility had suffered. He was no longer able to get to the communal areas on his own and, from the start of October, remained permanently confined to his room.

The week after the Leicester game, United lost 2-0 away at West Ham. At half-time, just after West Ham had scored their first goal, Dad had been in such a deep sleep that I'd stepped out of the room for a while, taking myself down the corridor to make a cup of tea in a small kitchenette area. In had walked one of Dad's nurses, who had made polite small talk for a while, asking how the football was going. I spent about ten minutes chatting to her in the end, giving her a concise backstory of Dad and I and how we'd gone to the football together for years before everything had caught up with him. I'd explained the lack of feeling I'd felt since he'd become more seriously ill, and how I'd ended up relinquishing my season ticket as a result. Aware that I knew my father was terminally ill, she'd asked if I was familiar with the term anticipatory grief. At the time I wasn't. As she began to explain, everything had made sense.

Anticipatory grief is the distress a person feels in the period before a loved one dies. Essentially, it's an awareness of a loss before the loss has actually happened, the way our minds attempt to cope and prepare ourselves. Not everyone experiences it, but it can occur in those who have, for example, seen someone close to them diagnosed with a form of dementia or Parkinson's. They grieve for the essence of the person they once were, even though, physically, that person is still there.

Everything I'd felt over the six or seven months leading up to that moment – the guilt, the frustration, the numbness – could be attributed in some way to the fact that, harsh though it seemed, the Dad I knew had in reality gone away long ago. Only remnants were left.

The Brighton match began. In his dimly lit room, Dad's eyes had remained open but heavy-lidded for the early minutes, blinking intermittently. His mouth hung open constantly – a new thing. Occasionally I'd pick up the sippy cup from his bedside table and, giving him a warning before I did so, drizzled a few drops of water inside his lips.

Fifteen miles away, United seemed to have started well, creating and spurning two or three early chances. Beneath the radio commentary the crowd were lively, which was a good sign. With a quarter of an hour gone they scored. The ball had fallen to Anthony Martial inside the Brighton box, left of goal. After one touch to set himself, he'd decided against a shot and slipped the ball back towards the edge of the box, where Andreas Pereira had wandered into an area of space. His shot had been drilled towards the bottom-right corner of the goal only to take a horrible deflection, deceiving the goalkeeper and dropping into the other corner.

'United have scored, Dad,' I said, softly. 'It's 1-0.'

He'd made another faint grunting noise after that, following it up with a chesty cough which I tried to pretend wasn't as bad as I'd thought it was.

Almost immediately United scored again, Scott McTominay bundling the ball over the line after Brighton had failed to head clear a free kick from just inside their half. I updated Dad. He raised his eyebrows slightly, which might have been totally unrelated but I decided to read as him being pleasantly surprised at a second goal coming so quickly.

There were no further goals in the first half. I think he fell asleep in the lull that followed the second goal but I couldn't be certain with his eyes not completely closed. I'd sneaked out, made a half-time cup of tea, then retaken my seat in time for the second half.

Dad didn't stir at all, looking so peaceful that I decided against telling him about Lewis Dunk pulling a goal back for Brighton. Soon after, Martial burst into the Brighton box but was forced too wide by the advancing goalkeeper. Turning back, he'd cut the ball to Marcus Rashford, who fired home via the underside of the bar.

I leaned over towards Dad, 'It's 3-1. Rashford.' This time, there came no grunt of acknowledgement or raising of his eyebrows. The drugs were doing their work. Dad was very definitely asleep, totally unaware that he'd missed what would prove to be the final United goal of his lifetime.

Half an hour later, the full-time whistle had sounded. United, a commentator announced, were now up to the dizzying heights of seventh in the Premier League table. I waited a few moments, then picked up my car keys from the side, stalling in the hope he might wake.

'I'm going now, Dad,' I'd told him, but nothing came back. I tugged his duvet up over his hands and left. The light was starting to fade as I got out to the car. Somewhere out of sight, a collared dove began to coo.

Chapter 16

1999

I'D LOVE to say I had a more captivating tale about the year United won the treble than I actually do, that Dad and I had been in the midst of the chaos behind the goal when Ole Gunnar Solskjaer prodded home the winner at the Camp Nou. We weren't though. There's no doubt in my mind that there are at least 40,000 other people with much better stories to tell about it than I do. Disappointing though it is, most of the decisive moments that took place towards the end of that season – the things that everyone talks about now – happened while we were watching from the couch in the living room or sitting at the kitchen table listening to crackling BBC radio commentary.

Junior football had continued to keep me away from nearly all the weekend games. Saturday morning matches in Wigan or Warrington or sometimes even Bolton meant returning home afterwards and then getting back out to Old Trafford in time for a 3pm kick-off hadn't been feasible. As it had been for the two seasons prior to that one, the games we did manage to attend were restricted almost entirely to the midweeks in the Champions League.

Regrettably, while so much of the bond Dad and I had was built upon our shared love of United, that season had also coincided with a period in which our relationship was as strained as it ever was. Some of it could be explained by my age: I'd turned 13 that season and, fitting all the stereotypes, was evolving into every inch the moody teenager, beginning to rebel and resent my parents, craving independence and distance from them.

It probably wasn't *just* the surge in hormones. The friction between Dad and I was exacerbated by the fact I'd ended up attending the same high school at which he and my mum taught, which, looking back, was a recipe for disaster. The freedom from them that I sought was never really possible. Worse still, it had brought constant scrutiny I simply wouldn't have received had I gone to another school.

I wasn't really badly behaved but had quickly come to discover that every time I put a foot wrong – be it by talking back to a teacher or underperforming in a test – Dad would get to know about it by the end of the week. When he did, I'd be sat down and reminded about how embarrassing it was for him and Mum and a full-blown argument would swiftly erupt.

Academically, I was relatively fine with the exception of maths. I wasn't naturally good with numbers and knew that I had to put the effort in to keep grades to a level which would keep me out of bother at home. *Knowing* I had to put the effort in and *putting* the effort in were two different things, however. When football had presented so many obvious distractions, algebraic equations and Pythagorus theory weren't really at the forefront of my mind.

In the autumn, I'd flunked a couple end of unit assessments, my score so low in one of them – which had fallen the day after I'd watched United earn a breathless 3-3 draw at home with Barcelona – that I was grounded for a couple of weeks. Beginning that year, cross words and groundings became a regular occurrence throughout my high-school years.

Watching the football with Dad was a time when, typically, the arguments would subside. Sadly, though, one of my main takeaways from that season of all seasons was that our journeys to and from Old Trafford on those incredible European nights were often made in silence, the widening distance between us becoming more apparent.

After seeing off Polish champions ŁKS Łódź in a qualifier on a balmy late-summer evening at Old Trafford, a nightmarish group stage draw had pitted United with Barcelona, Bayern Munich and Danish champions Brøndby. They made it out, but on the surface had scraped through with only two wins – both convincing ones against Brøndby. Qualification for the quarter-finals came only by taking one of the two best runners-up spots. Crucially though, United had come through four games with Barça and Bayern unbeaten, which was seen as a massive positive. The away game in the Camp Nou – another 3-3 draw – had eliminated Barça from the competition on home soil and felt like a significant yardstick for those who remembered the 4-0 mauling United had received in the same setting four years earlier. It was only after all that, as winter relaxed its grip and European football returned, that my most vivid memories of the season kick in.

None of the big, high-pressure games were particularly enjoyable. The bit *after* them was, when victory was secured, but the matches themselves were all filled with the same unbearable, nerve-shredding tension.

Inter Milan at home in the first leg of the quarter-final had been the start of it. The first half was fine, played in one of the best atmospheres I've ever experienced at Old Trafford. Dwight Yorke had headed home a swinging David Beckham cross early on, then the two combined in similar fashion as half-time approached to double the lead. Dad had been cautious at the break though, warning that if Inter got an away goal, United would be in bother. This played on my mind all through the second half.

Inter, realising they'd need something to take back to Milan, were better after the break and the raucous atmosphere of the first 45 minutes became accordingly subdued. Iván Zamorano, wearing a 1+8 on his back after Ronaldo had taken Inter's number nine shirt, had drawn a decent save from Peter Schmeichel; Henning Berg, on as a sub for Ronny Johnsen at the back, produced a goal-line clearance which felt as much a seminal moment as anything in the tie.

Clinging on to a clean sheet had felt massive and, from that night onwards, treble talk had started to bubble up.

Ronaldo had been absent at Old Trafford but returned for the second leg in the San Siro. Inter went ahead on the night after an hour and had United on the ropes for a while after it. Dad, I remember, had silently left the room for a few minutes as the pressure grew. Inter's efforts to level the tie gradually began to fizzle out as full time approached and Dad had regained enough composure to come back into the room, remaining standing when he did.

With United regathering a measure of control, Gary Neville slung a high ball into the box for Andy Cole, who nodded it down towards an unmarked Paul Scholes. He'd kept his head to apply the finish, an away goal which, with minutes remaining, had effectively ended the tie. Dad, Chris and I leapt around the living room, the confused dog joining in as we did. Finally, as we settled down, Dad had felt relaxed enough to retake a seat.

In the semi, United were reacquainted with Juventus. Again, the home leg came first, but the fixture at Old Trafford hadn't been a bit like the Inter game. After Beckham had gone close with an early free kick, Juve, with Edgar Davids and Zinedine Zidane controlling things from midfield, had been better. They deservedly took the lead when Antonio

Conte was played through after 25 minutes, Old Trafford falling totally silent but for the couple of thousand Italians over in the away end.

Dad had become increasingly agitated as the game had run on. Juve were better that night, in truth. They might not have created many chances but they'd kept the ball well and masterfully stifled United. They were also wily and streetwise enough to draw fouls and eat up a few seconds in those moments where it felt United were building momentum. Dad had ranted at the referee for repeatedly failing to clamp down on their antics, then snapped at a man in the crowd who'd decided it best to leave ten minutes early to beat the traffic outside. The game was slipping away. He knew it, and so did everyone else.

Stoppage time arrived. With the crowd all on their feet, Beckham hooked a hopeful, lobbed cross into the area. Juve failed to deal with it and it had eventually fallen kindly at the feet of Ryan Giggs, who lashed an equaliser into the roof of the goal. Old Trafford exploded. Juve would still be favourites in Turin, but as we left for home there was renewed belief that United might still find a way.

By the time of the second leg, Giggs's solo goal against Arsenal had seen United into the FA Cup Final. Dad had relented on his refusal to purchase Sky Sports, but stopped short of buying the most expensive package. The Arsenal semi and the following replay had been on Sky Sports 2, which we didn't have. Instead, we gathered around the table in the kitchen, where the only radio in the house was situated, and listened in. We were weary by extra time. The score remained 1-1 and Dennis Bergkamp had seen Schmeichel save a last-gasp penalty, but after Roy Keane had been sent off, that had only seemed to delay the inevitable. Arsenal would surely do enough with a numerical advantage with another half an hour to play.

The minutes ticked on and a faint hope that United might force penalties began to grow. Then Giggs had seized on Patrick Vieira's wayward pass and began to run. The time it took for him to reach the Arsenal penalty area had been no more than five seconds; to us, relying only on radio commentary, it had felt like minutes. Alan Green's voice on the BBC had steadily become more strained and high-pitch as Giggs approached the goal, almost a squeak by the time he struck the ball past David Seaman.

A week later, United flew to Turin. We assumed our usual positions in the living room and watched on as, with barely ten minutes gone, they looked to have blown it.

Zidane played an early corner short, exchanged a one-two with Angelo Di Livio and whipped a cross towards the back post where Filippo Inzaghi had got the wrong side of Gary Neville; 1-0. It got worse. Inzaghi was fed the ball in the corner of United's area soon afterwards, where Jaap Stam was quickly across to get tight to him. Engineering just enough space to get the ball from under his feet, Inzaghi attempted to drive it back across goal. Stam stretched out a leg to block it but the ball ricocheted off his heel and into the turf, looping up, ominously. Schmeichel beaten, it dropped into the corner of the goal. 'That's it,' Dad had sighed. 'You don't concede goals like that and go through.'

By half-time he'd changed his tune. Keane's header had halved the deficit on the night, then Cole combined with Beckham on the right to pick out Yorke, who nodded in the second away goal. Having accepted United's fate after the Inzaghi brace, the nerves had ratcheted up after that, only settling in the dying seconds. Schmeichel pumped the ball downfield only for Juve's defenders to nod it to Yorke. Bursting through a gap between two home players, he was brought down by Angelo Peruzzi in the Juve goal. A penalty would have almost certainly have been awarded had Cole not been there to follow up and slide home the winner. Bayern Munich awaited in a first European Cup Final since 1968. The treble, somehow, was possible.

I'd worked out soon after the win over Juve that the final would fall slap bang in the middle of exam week, which, given how the earlier tests had gone, wasn't ideal if I wanted to see any daylight over the six-week summer holiday. To make matters worse, it was later announced that the maths tests would be done the morning after the final. I still had a couple of weeks to go when I realised this and – laughably – convinced myself I'd eke out enough time to revise. Had the end to the season been less eventful, I might have been more disciplined in that regard, but with the league going down to the final game and the FA Cup Final being played a week later, there had been ample reasons to procrastinate.

United cleared the first two hurdles, flying to Barcelona after beating Newcastle at Wembley. I'd been intensely jealous of a couple of the lads I knew who'd got tickets and bunked off school for a few days to go and watch it.

The build-up in the media was already in full swing by the Monday morning. Granada Reports and GMTV had seemed to run entire shows consisting of speaking to Barcelona-bound supporters outside Manchester Airport departure lounge; the *Evening News* had seemed to stick out a new special edition preview supplement every six hours.

Wednesday came. The hours dragged until kick-off was finally close and we took up our usual positions in front of the TV, the sense of occasion underlined by Dad, who never usually had a drink on a school night, cracking open one of a specially purchased six-pack of lager.

For reasons I can't explain, my memories of the game itself are almost nonexistent. Maybe it's down to the stress or how engrossed I'd been in it; perhaps it's because, after watching the highlights back so many times in the years that have since passed, it's harder to remember how it was the first time it happened. That, I find, is usually the way of it when you watch a match on TV. It's easier to remember more when you're inside the stadium with your own unique perspective of it all.

Mario Basler scored an early free kick. Dad was aggrieved that it had even been awarded in the first place, then annoyed at Schmeichel for leaving the side of his goal in which the ball had been placed so open. That was largely the extent of it for the first half.

Into the second, Dad, on his third or fourth can by then, had grown even more frustrated at United's inability to get going. When Jesper Blomqvist had lifted the ball over the Bayern bar after being picked out by a deep Giggs cross from the right, he'd slammed an empty can down on to the floor. Bayern had come close to extending their lead after that. Mehmet Scholl lofted a chip over Schmeichel from the edge of the area which, to this day, still looks as though it's goalbound. It wasn't, and pinged back off the post and into Schmeichel's arms.

Towards the end, at about the time when the board had gone up for stoppage time, Dad had mellowed and become strangely fatalistic. Bracing Chris and I for the disappointment to come, he'd turned to us.

'Whatever happens, they've done us proud this year, lads,' he'd said, probably slightly pissed by then. 'There's always next year.'

And then United won a corner. Ron Atkinson, on co-commentary duty for ITV, had said something about Peter Schmeichel coming up.

Five minutes later, it was over. The treble sealed. Football, bloody hell. Before the trophy presentation, Dad had put a hand on my shoulder so that I looked at him. 'Come on,' he said, nodding towards the door. 'You've got some revising to do.' Just as I'd been about to leave the room and head upstairs, he'd started to laugh. 'Sit down. That can wait.'

On Thursday, 27 May 1999, I failed an end-of-year maths test.

Chapter 17

Saying goodbye

THE DAY after I'd sat at Dad's bedside and listened to United beat Brighton, I'd woken early to the sound of Ethan crying. It was a Monday. I took him downstairs around six, leaving Lauren to lie in until her alarm went off and she had to get ready for work. An hour later, after he'd settled into watching some CBeebies and I'd fed him a few spoonfuls of his breakfast, Lauren had called down to say my phone was ringing. It was my mum, she said, and I braced myself.

Mum sounded panicked. 'The home have been on to me, love,' she said. 'We might need to be there today. I think something might be happening.'

I put the phone down, hastily cancelled my plans and arranged to make my way over once the rush-hour traffic had eased. After doing that, I'd called Mum again to be sure of some of the details I didn't absorb the first time round. The home, it transpired, had called her – which in itself wasn't a good sign – just before seven o'clock. The staff assigned to Dad's floor overnight had grown concerned that he'd developed a cough, possibly the same spluttering cough I'd tried to ignore during the game the previous afternoon. On top of that, he'd eaten no more food since I'd left him. The nurse on the phone put it to Mum gently that the time had come to contact his children and anyone else who might wish to arrange a visit – 'soon'.

As a family, we had known by then that death was coming, but no amount of preparation and acceptance makes that moment of realisation that it's imminent any easier. Before that Monday morning we'd optimistically assumed we were still dealing in weeks, not days. We'd all read up on what the indicators were that it was close and were satisfied enough that while he ticked a few things on the list – the downturn in appetite, the near-constant sleep – there were still plenty more unchecked. It was, looking back, a final flicker of denial.

I'd arrived at the home at around ten, rushing through the reception area to find the door to Dad's room closed. Inside, Mum and Chris were sitting beneath the window on the far side of his bed, the curtains behind them still drawn.

Dad had been awake. Weak, but alert enough to turn his head slightly towards me as I approached the bed. His face appeared to have somehow changed in the 15 hours or so that had passed since I was last with him: thinner still, more yellow. His eyes were partially open again, but totally glazed and lifeless. I was sure that his vision had gone. As I processed this, I couldn't bring myself to force out the usual hello. Mum had seemed to realise this and stepped in to explain that I'd arrived. There was no response, only the muffled sound of a TV in one of the rooms across the corridor. For what might have been an hour or so, nobody spoke, the silence occasionally punctuated by Dad's newly developed cough.

Later there came a knock on the door: one of the nurses, asking would we mind if she shaved Dad's face. We watched as she gently lathered up his cheeks and throat, then scraped away the foam with a razor blade, all while holding normal, everyday conversation with Mum. After his shave, Mum had dabbed Dad's face with a warm flannel and poured a few drips of water on to his lips. He'd begun to groan with pain soon after this. The nurse returned and administered a dose of painkillers which seemed to take hold quickly, allowing him to drop off into a peaceful sleep again, the gentle rise and fall of his chest beneath the duvet the only clue he was still with us.

We continued to watch over him for a while longer until I'd got up to go and make a cup of coffee. When I did, Mum followed me out into the corridor afterwards and updated me. Dad wasn't expected to see out the week. Things were moving at such a rate that 72 hours now seemed optimistic. After she'd arrived earlier in the morning, a doctor had spoken to her about putting him on a medicine I'd never heard of before, called midazolam. This would help with his agitation as the end drew near.

Towards the end of the afternoon, Dad's cough had started to weaken and evolve into a faint gurgling sound from somewhere deep inside his throat. This quickly became more pronounced as time ticked on and I'd recognised immediately what it was. Nearly everything I'd read on the signs that someone was close to dying had mentioned a 'death rattle' – a distinctive noise made when saliva and mucus in the throat and parts of the airways builds up and the person is too weak to be able to clear it with a cough.

Evening came. Through the narrow crack between the curtains in his room, I could see the light go. My sisters arrived. Mum told me the midazolam was due to be administered soon, after we'd all had chance to speak to him. Because it would relax him and induce sleepiness, we were warned that there was a chance he may be too weak and could slip away quite quickly once it had been given to him. Mum relayed this information to everyone in the room individually, seeing if anyone had any objections. Nobody did. She returned to the chair next to Dad, taking his hand.

At that moment had come a final burst of perception, as if Dad knew what was coming. Having barely moved in hours, he'd suddenly summoned enough energy to attempt to lift Mum's hand to his mouth and attempt to kiss it. Pathetically, he'd been too weak and missed her hand. After that, everyone bar Mum had left the room.

One by one, we'd each gone back into the room on our own to speak to Dad alone, to say our goodbyes. Dad had been in a deep sleep when it came to my turn. I honestly can't remember now if he'd been given the midazolam already, but seeing how still and serene he'd been in that moment, I'd imagine he had. At first, I'd said nothing, trying not to cry on the off chance he could hear and understand. Finally, after composing myself enough, I'd taken his hand and pushed out a few words, thanking him for all he'd done for me in my life. I talked a lot about the holidays when Chris and I were kids – to Switzerland, to Italy, to the Black Forest. I apologised for the times we'd constantly argued when I was a teenager, how I'd not always been perfect when I was at school.

Finally – inevitably – it had come back to football and United. I told him of how grateful I was to have shared those innumerable afternoons and evenings at Old Trafford by his side, how I badly wished we still had a few more years so he could see go along and accompany his grandson for his first game. I recounted some of the goals and moments he'd mentioned during his final few months, probably in the hope of it triggering a final, miraculous response from him, if only a gentle squeeze of the hand. It didn't. After a pause, I told him I loved him, kissed him on the forehead, and left the room.

That night I slept lightly and in patches, waking regularly to see if I'd somehow missed a crucial call. Morning finally came without any updates. After snatching at some breakfast, I set out again, back to the home. Nothing had changed when

I got there. Dad lay in an identical position to the one I'd left him in, his upper body propped up at a 45-degree angle. Mum was already back at his bedside. Chris arrived soon after, the three of us keeping watch for the rest of the morning.

By midday, we noticed his hands and feet had become cold. The skin around his ankles had become mottled, tinged with purple.

One of the nurses came by to examine him and, after doing so, advised us all to go out and get something to eat. His breathing was steady, she'd pointed out. Even the horrendous gurgling noise he'd begun to make the previous afternoon seemed to have waned.

The three of us drove into Warrington and silently picked at some food in a coffee shop, phones laid face up on the table in front of us, just in case. Back we went, braced for another long stint at his bedside.

When we returned, though, something had changed. Two of the nurses had been at his bedside when we entered his room. When I saw them I wondered if we'd missed him while we were away. One of the nurses left the room immediately; the one who remained explaining that his breathing appeared to have quickened.

'This doesn't mean he's in distress,' she told us, sympathetically. 'He's peaceful. He's in no pain at all now.'

We reassumed our positions, waiting. For what felt like about an hour, Dad's breathing seemed to steadily accelerate even more, becoming increasingly shallow as it did. At just after 4pm, it stopped entirely and we wondered if that was it. As we looked at each other, his body had jolted and the breathing had started up again. This happened three times, the gap between breaths becoming progressively longer each time it did.

Then, with the digital alarm clock opposite his bed reading 4:42, his breathing stopped and we waited again.

This time, nothing happened. The remaining colour in his face slowly drained away and Mum began to say a prayer.

I summoned a nurse. She came in, held his wrist and checked his throat for a pulse.

'I'm very sorry,' she said. 'I'm going to give you some privacy for a while.'

Chapter 18

2008

BY THE time we poured out of one of the arena exit doors, it was gone midnight. The streets were heaving, red shirts spilling off the pavements and into the roads. Taxis incessantly sounded their horns, some in celebration, others at the hordes blocking their path. Clusters of the crowds sung 'Campeones', others belted out 'Viva Ronaldo' as they drunkenly twirled scarves around their heads.

On to the bottom of Deansgate, the celebrations seemed to intensify as the pubs emptied. Flags waved, red smoke billowed from a dozen smoke grenades.

I'd seen the missed calls by then. Three of them, all from Dad. I'd call back later, I told myself.

For a short while, I'd toyed with going to Moscow for the 2008 Champions League Final. The semi-final against Barcelona – particularly the second leg, when United held on to a precarious lead with fingernails – had been sheer agony. When it was over, I'd convinced myself I deserved to go to Russia for the final as rewards for coming through it.

The next morning, I'd quickly realised there was no chance of this happening. I'd sat my final exam at uni in Leeds that month and had spent my final weeks as a student doing what most students do: frittering away the last of my loan on nights out filled with watered-down pints and cheap vodka Red Bulls. The soaring cost of flights to and from Moscow – even when taking the most creative and obscenely lengthy route – was well beyond my budget, and that was before I had even thought about accommodation and how I would manage to get my hands on a ticket.

Instead, then, a different plan was formulated. The MEN Arena was screening the final. Along with my brother and a few mates who I'd gone to games with, we bought some tickets.

I watched in a bar in Headingley as United wrapped up the Premier League away at Wigan at the weekend, then, on the day of the final, caught the first off-peak train to Piccadilly, managing to avoid the ticket conductor. Dad had called when the train had reached Stalybridge and asked if I wanted to watch it with him at home. I told him I'd made plans with the lads and he'd offered to pick a few of us up after full time somewhere near the cathedral.

In Manchester, I'd met a couple of others at the station then crossed the road to the Manchester University campus, where, in a windowless student union bar, we loaded ourselves up on £1.60 pints of lager until mid-afternoon.

Half-cut, we'd wandered over to Chinatown for a an all-you-can-eat buffet for dinner, then we went into a Wetherspoons off Piccadilly Gardens for a few more rounds. A couple of hours before kick-off we made our way down Market Street, assuming we'd reach the arena in ample time to get a decent spot. Inside, the seats in the bottom tier had been opened up, creating a giant U shape around the huge screen, which stood in the middle. Most of the seats had already been taken by then, so we settled for a standing position at the bottom.

The game began, United starting better, deservedly taking the lead when Wes Brown's cross found Cristiano Ronaldo, who out-leaped Michael Essien to thump a header beyond

Petr Čech. For a minute or two after that it was bedlam all around us, being inside the arena amplifying the noise. Memories for the hour or so after that are, perhaps owed to the all-day bender, somewhat foggy. United should have gone two up. Ronaldo found Carlos Tevez, whose diving header was saved by Čech. John Terry scrambled the ball away to the edge of the area, where Carrick's drilled effort was again palmed over by Čech. Minutes later, Wayne Rooney crafted enough space to cross from the right. Tevez was again the intended target but could only get studs to the ball, which zipped out for a goal kick.

With half-time approaching, Chelsea scraped an equaliser. Rio Ferdinand tackled Florent Malouda midway through the United half but the loose ball had fallen to Essien. From distance he attempted a shot, which ricocheted off Nemanja Vidić's heel and then Ferdinand's back, dropping kindly to Frank Lampard, who stroked it past Edwin van der Sar; 1-1. At that moment, a girl standing to the right of us had vomited all over the floor and was escorted away by a friend.

Chelsea were better in the second half. Didier Drogba clipped the outside of the post from distance; Michael Ballack went close. The game evened itself out over extra time; Ryan Giggs, on as a sub, had a shot cleared off the line by Terry; Lampard thudded a shot against the underside of United's bar. In the dying embers of the game Drogba was sent off for slapping Vidić. There wasn't enough time remaining in play for United to make the advantage count, but it's entirely possible Chelsea might have scored all five of their first penalties had he been available to take one.

Naturally, the start of the shoot-out was tense. When Ronaldo saw his penalty pushed away by Čech, I resigned myself to the defeat. He'd been phenomenal that season, picking up where he'd left off in 2006/07 and somehow managing to up his game further still, amassing an obscene goal tally. By the turn of the year you'd expected him to score in every game and, more often than not, he did. It would have been just like football to make it so that his very last kick of that campaign ended up costing United a European Cup.

Mercifully, up had stepped Terry for the crucial penalty, adjusting his captain's armband as he walked towards the goal. Score and it was done: Chelsea were champions of Europe. Then came the slip, the ball striking the post and flitting off to the right, out of shot. Cue bedlam all around – so much so that a man close by us forgot his bearings and went skidding through the puddle of sick which had remained undisturbed on the floor since Lampard's equaliser, like an unintended Terry tribute act.

Strangely, Terry's miss and the burst of unexpected euphoria seemed to rid me of my nerves. Though four more penalties were taken after it, I'd suddenly felt unnaturally calm and relaxed given the high stakes, as if destiny had decided it was United's night. Others, I think, shared that feeling, because when Nicolas Anelka's face had appeared on the big screen, a small cheer had gone up as if the audience knew what was coming next. It would be fitting that he – a former Liverpool, City and Arsenal player – would ultimately hand United the trophy. Up he stepped, run-up short, penalty struck tamely and at just the right height for Van der Sar to push it away. United ruled Europe.

Before the trophy presentation, when the initial explosion of noise had subsided, I'd pulled out my phone to call Dad but quickly abandoned my attempts to speak to him. The reception was awful and the noise inside the arena wouldn't have made for a smooth phone call.

Out into the night we had eventually gone, along Deansgate, up towards the town hall and back through to Piccadilly Gardens. By one, I was sobering up and found time to speak to Dad, who by then was waiting in his car down near Cathedral Gardens. By the time we'd reached him he'd been waiting an hour, listening to the reaction from Moscow on the radio.

After dropping off the last of my mates in Leigh, we'd talked about the game and it had dawned on me that he'd watched the entire thing alone. I suddenly felt horrendously guilty.

'I've recorded all the stuff after the game from MUTV,' he said. 'There's beers in the fridge if you fancy staying up and watching some more of it?'

I really didn't – the first signs of a hangover headache were already beginning to pulse – but agreed to nonetheless. We'd sat up until the break of dawn watching it, talking about the game and next season. At one point they'd shown footage from the MEN Arena of the moment Anelka's penalty was saved. There, in the middle of the tumult, were the lads and I.

'I'd rather have been there than watching it here,' he'd said, sipping from his can.

I'd fallen asleep on the couch, waking sometime in late morning with a raging hangover which didn't clear until the next day.

That night was an epiphany moment for me. Not so much being in the MEN and watching the game, but the couple of hours after I got home where I fought off sleep so Dad and I could watch every last drop of the post-match coverage.

For a long time, beginning in that period where Dad and I were near constantly at each other's throats, I'd preferred going to matches with mates. By the time I'd left school and particularly when I was away at uni when the student mindset was deeply ingrained, I'd go to a game and then off out after it, having a few drinks in 42s off Deansgate. Dad and I still went to the football together but it wasn't as commonplace as it had once been.

That time between finishing school and your early 20s is an awkward one. You're barely an adult and still stuck finding out who you really are and forging your own identity. Naturally, I think, you try and distance yourself from your parents as part of that process. This was definitely the case with me – perhaps more so given my experience of high school – and it undoubtedly extended to the company I'd choose to keep on matchdays for a few years, with Dad very much becoming the backup option.

At the end of that phase, you're enough of your own person to feel comfortable in embracing the similarities you have with your parents. That, at the end of uni, was where I was. I'd found myself reflecting lots about when I was a kid and Dad and I would go to Old Trafford together – yearning to do it again. I'm certain some of it might have been that his cancer diagnosis was still quite recent and raw and, as a result, I'd become aware of his mortality and how little time we might have left ahead of us.

From the night of the Moscow final forward, I only ever really wanted to go to games with him, to savour the experience of doing so. Mainly because I knew a day would come where I wouldn't be able to.

I only wish that our timing could have been better. The next season, we'd managed to get to Old Trafford regularly, catching the end of Ronaldo's first spell at the club before the pressure from Real Madrid became unsurmountable and he was sold for a world record fee. By the time we were going to every home match again, though, it had felt like United were slowly on the way down. Because of Fergie, they were able to remain competitive for a few years more and win a couple more titles, but it hadn't felt quite the same. The rate at which other clubs were improving – namely City, with their enormous backing from Abu Dhabi – meant what happened after Fergie retired was almost inevitable. Without him, the Glazers' ownership and the bewildering incompetence of some of those trusted to make big footballing decisions saw United struggle to adjust, first under David Moyes, then Louis van Gaal and José Mourinho. As a result, so much of the final years I spent going to United with Dad were set against the backdrop of expensively assembled, mediocre-at-best football.

And yet, in many ways it didn't matter.

As I've touched on earlier in this book, the older you get, going to watch the football becomes less about your team winning or losing and more about who you're watching with. So much of what makes it special isn't what takes place in the 90 minutes on the pitch, but what you talk about during the car journeys there and back, the walks to and from the turnstiles or over a pint after full time. I learnt more about my dad during that period than I'd ever done, often about parts of his life he'd never opened up about before. Because we were able to go to the game together so regularly, our bond became as strong as it ever was in those final years. Grateful though I am for all that, the sad byproduct was that as time went on it was at the football I learnt to chart his deterioration – first physically, with his knee crumbling like a pack of battered digestive biscuits, then, later on, with his fading memory.

Supporting a football team, I think, becomes altogether more difficult to step away from when it's been passed on to you by a parent. Once they've got you in, there's an onus placed upon on you that you don't get out again – at least not fully. Going along with them for so long also gives you that awareness of how time passes, of how no one outruns age. *They* take *you* to your first game. In the end, it's *you* taking *them*.

One of the last truly great nights we had at Old Trafford came on a Monday in late April 2013, when United beat Aston Villa to win the title back from City. Robin van Persie had scored a hat-trick to make certain of the result with little over half an hour played.

In the dying moments of the game, a chant of 'stand up for the champions' had risen up from the Stretford End and circulated around the stadium. Everyone stood accordingly, joining in with the chant.

Lauren and I were engaged by then, planning our wedding the next year. Perhaps sensing that there wouldn't be many nights left like this, Dad had put an arm around me just before the game reached full time and, completely out of character for him, had uttered something about how happy he was that he'd got to share such moments with me.

'You and Lauren need to hurry up,' he'd said, finally. 'I want to be able to bring my grandkids along to nights like this.'

The whistle blew.

Chapter 19

Programmes in a drawer

THE MORNING after I watched Dad die, I woke early. In an attempt to keep my mind occupied I threw myself into boxing off some of the jobs his passing had created.

Firstly, Lauren had driven me to the other side of Warrington and a small GP surgery I'd passed countless times on the way to Dad's home yet never once noticed. I gave my name at the front desk and explained why I was there and was hastily shown to an empty room down a corridor, away from the already-crammed waiting room. Before long a doctor entered, offered his condolences and then pulled out a piece of paper from a file on the desk: the death certificate. The cause of death, he explained, was metastatic prostate cancer, which I remember thinking had somewhat unfairly told only part of the story of what he'd gone through towards the end. The doctor slotted the certificate inside a plain white envelope as he explained the formalities of registering the death.

From the surgery, I'd insisted on going back to the home to clear the room of Dad's belongings. To my mind, that process would only become more difficult the longer it was left, when the initial numbness that grief brings had begun to burn away.

At the door to the home I was greeted by some of the nurses who had cared for Dad towards the end but hadn't been on shift the previous evening. They'd offered hugs and said how sorry they were before leaving us to get on with the task at hand.

The room felt immediately different when I entered. For the first time in weeks, the curtains were pulled back and daylight had poured in through the window. The smell had changed, too, as if it had already been given a thorough clean .in preparation for its next occupant. The bed where Dad had lay had been stripped and pushed back against a wall. A single white rose had been placed on the mattress where he'd lay, the sight of which almost enough to tug me out of the desensitised state that gripped me.

We got to it, beginning by opening the wardrobe and drawers, bundling all of his clothes into a couple of large bin liners and trying to ignore the occasional faint waft of the aftershave he used to wear as we went about it. The clothes eventually bagged up and loaded into the boot of the car, I'd gone back to collect the other items dotted around on the windowsill and on top of the other surfaces. There wasn't much: a lamp, an old digital clock, a few picture books of the Swiss Alps and various photographs and albums. One of the pictures was an unframed black-and-white image of him during his Warrington Town days, the corners slightly frayed and bent over time. With a ball between his boots, Dad sat front and centre of a team photo, fresh-faced, hair dark and long. Knowing how it had ended, the relentless cruelty of his final weeks, seeing this version of him – so full of life and in his physical prime – had been jarring and difficult to look at. Into a cardboard box it went, along with the other items.

Just as we'd seemed to clear the last of it, I'd remembered to check the drawer of a bedside table in the far corner of the room. Beneath a few pairs of socks had been a pile of four or five programmes I'd brought him back from the games I'd attended towards the end of last season. Along with some of his other belongings, they'd followed Dad over from the hospital in May before being stuffed in the drawer and completely forgotten about. I'd glanced at each of the covers, remembering as I did where in his slow decline Dad had been up to when I'd presented each of them to him. I'd started to feel a hint of anger as I flicked through them.

In that moment, football – the idea of your entire life revolving around a one-way bond with players and managers who'll never even know your name, all of the inherent petty rivalries that come with it – had felt more futile than ever before. This wasn't just the steadily building apathy I'd felt towards United since the Paris Saint-Germain game, but something more intense. I wondered if, without Dad, it could ever mean the same as it had before. How, when I'd witnessed first-hand what *real* pain had looked like, the look on Dad's face when the morphine had begun to wear off, could I ever give a shit about getting rolled over in a derby again? Would Liverpool finally winning a league title really be quite so unbearable when, towards the end of his life, my own father had all but forgotten I existed?

'What do you want to do with them?' Lauren had called over.

'I think I'll leave them here,' I replied. And we left.

The funeral took place two weeks later at a crematorium nearby the home. The hearse carrying Dad had pulled up outside my parents' home and Lauren and I had got into the back of one of the following cars as it made its way through central Warrington, passing Owen Street where the long-since levelled home where Dad had first lived had once stood, then Cantilever Park, where he'd played for Warrington Town. Along with family and old work colleagues, some of his former team-mates had also turned up to pay their respects.

The eulogy was delivered by Mike, one of his oldest friends and an even more ardent United supporter than Dad.

As the service concluded a curtain was drawn around the coffin and, to the soundtrack of 'In My Life' by the Beatles, a video montage showing a stream of pictures of Dad at various stages of his life played on a screen at the front of the room.

Somewhere in the background, United had plundered on inconsistently under Ole Gunnar Solskjaer after the international break, beating Tottenham at home and then City away before dropping points when they hosted Everton and losing away at relegation-threatened Watford. I couldn't bring myself to watch the games on TV for a few weeks and knocked back a couple of offers from friends to go to Old Trafford. Had it not been for my job, I wonder if I'd have paid any attention to football whatsoever.

In early February, I'd gone back to Old Trafford for the first time to cover the ceremony for the Munich anniversary. The setup was the same as it always was: a small stage erected at the foot of the memorial plaque and the image of the Babes lining up before the game in Belgrade. It was the first time I'd looked at it since two years earlier, when Dad had surprised me by reciting all of their names.

To the right of the stage, we were directed to a small fenced-off square reserved for those in the media, directly opposite where Solskjaer and other club representatives were lining up. As we set up, a large crowd began to assemble in a huge horseshoe around the stage. Suddenly, I'd heard a familiar voice calling my name, somewhere over to the left. I looked up and saw Frank grinning at me as he leaned against one of the temporary railings segregating the crowd from the stage. I'd shouted hello and asked how he was getting on.

'Fine,' he'd replied. 'How's your dad doing?' *Oh.*

I didn't answer his question, promising I'd catch up with him after the ceremony had finished. By the time it had, I couldn't find him as the crowds dispersed.

United's form had started to improve by the time of the memorial, helped by the arrival of Bruno Fernandes. In early March they hosted City in the second league derby of the season, the first game I'd felt compelled to watch since Dad had died. Anthony Martial had given United the lead after half an hour following a smartly taken Fernandes free kick. Then, right at the death, Ederson in the City goal had hurried the ball out of his feet in a bid to start one last attempt to find an equaliser. His pass out to a team-mate was intercepted by Scott McTominay, who fired the ball into the empty net from distance, sealing the win. There, for the first time in a long time, I'd felt a flicker of excitement. Just for a second, I'd imagined what it was like up in and around our old seats, how Dad and I might have celebrated had we been in the thick of it all. But then the game had ended and the feeling soon passed. I had no real desire to go back to Old Trafford anytime soon. I was certain of that. Doing so would still be too painful and I was comfortable with the thought of staying away for a while, letting time heal all that had happened. Only when the time was right, when I had a good enough reason to, would I return.

Chapter 20

Ethan

OVER TWO years would pass before I had a good enough reason.

Before Ethan was born, I'd vowed not to be one of those parents who deliberately imposes their own interests on their kids in the hope that they grow to love the same things. It was important, I told myself, for him to discover his own things to be passionate about and my duty as a father was to support and encourage that. I really did try.

For a while, it seemed to be going well enough. I didn't tell him to like Thomas the Tank Engine, he chose that himself. It was the same with his year-long fixation with tractors and then the dinosaur phase which, as I write this four years later, shows no sign of coming to an end. All that was him. Football – more specifically United – wasn't on his radar at all for at least the first three and a half years of his life.

Ethan adored his Grandad Dave. It will always make me profoundly sad that Dad wasn't in his life for longer than he actually was. When Dad had first been taken into hospital, I'd visit my parents' house with Ethan to check in on Mum. Without fail, he'd totter off into the back room and check to see if Dad was in his usual spot in front of the TV. This didn't stop until around the time of his death, when he'd seemed to finally accept that he wasn't living in the house any more.

When Dad had eventually settled into the nursing home, Ethan had enjoyed visiting him a few times. About a month before the end, though, Lauren and I decided it was probably best we put a stop to that. It was unlikely, given his age, that he would ever remember Dad, but on the off chance he did, we didn't want him to remember the way he was in those final weeks.

Not long after Dad had died, Lauren and I discovered we were expecting a second child. A couple of months after that – immediately after United had won the derby at Old Trafford in early March – everything had shut down as the world was plunged into the Covid-19 pandemic. Those two things had meant that, through spring and summer, Ethan and I had spent more time together than I could ever have dreamed.

The days were long, Ethan often waking at the crack of dawn. Sometimes we would go out in the back garden, where I had assembled a small plastic goal frame, and kick a ball about. Whenever he'd kick the ball into the goal, I'd pick him up and spin him round as a celebration. He'd enjoy that for a few minutes before his mind would wander to other things. Most of the days, when the weather allowed it, we had gone out for walks across the fields and through the woodland near to our home, taking a packed lunch with us to eat somewhere along the way. That, to him, was a big adventure and something he looked forward to.

I was conscious that as he grew, tiny head filling with more and more information about the world around him, he would forget about Dad. In a slightly desperate bid to try and delay that inevitability, I had made sure I spoke about him wherever appropriate. The walks we would go on were often to places Dad had taken me as a kid and I would tell him little stories about those times in the faint hope it kept him in his mind. On one of the walks, he spontaneously asked where Grandad Dave had gone.

'Does he not live at Nana's house now?' he asked, and I told him no, that he'd gone somewhere else, somewhere happy. He'd seemed to accept that.

In the middle of that summer, football had started up again with Premier League fixtures played behind closed doors. They were televised and, partly because watching football had broken up the monotony of lockdown life, I'd settled back into a routine of watching United on a regular basis again.

When the games were on, Ethan would occasionally potter into the room, miniature t-rex or triceratops in hand, and glance at the TV. At three and a half he had no real concept of what I was watching but was able to make a connection between what was on the screen and the way the two of us would sometimes kick a ball around in the back yard.

Just before Robyn, Ethan's little sister, had been born, United played one of their final home games of the season against Southampton. He'd briefly sat down beside me while it was on.

'This is at Old Trafford,' I'd said, seizing the opportunity. 'That's where I used to go with Grandad Dave to watch United. It's enormous.'

'Is he there now?' he'd replied.

'No.'

'Is it bigger than a long neck dinosaur?'

He'd seemed mildly impressed when I told him it was, but then quickly wandered off back to his toys. And that, for a while, was the extent of his interest.

Ethan turned four at the start of the next year and took wonderfully to his role as a big brother. With the world gradually returning to normal, he started a nursery affiliated with a local church school in the spring. As the weather began to warm, I'd sometimes walk him home at the end of each day. On one of these walks he asked if Grandad Dave now lived in place called Heaven. I was taken aback, but figured the question was likely prompted by something he'd heard at nursery. I told him yes, he did, and he followed up by asking if there were any shops there. I didn't know that.

Another question: 'What did Grandad Dave look like?'

And it dawned on me then that he'd probably forgotten him.

United finished the 2020/21 season a distant second to City. After dropping out of the Champions League group stages, they reached the Europa League Final in Gdańsk, somehow losing via a mammoth penalty shoot-out to Villarreal. I'd long since fallen back into a comfortable routine of watching all the games on TV by then, content to observe from a distance.

Ethan still hadn't fully grasped what football was. He knew there was a goal, he understood the objective was to kick the ball *into* the goal and he'd become aware that there was a man called Marcus Rashford who played for a team called 'United'. That was about it.

I can't pinpoint when or how he became aware of Rashford. All I know is, towards the end of that season, whenever he'd seen that a game was on, he'd habitually ask which team Rashford was on – as if no game of football could ever be permitted to take place without a Marcus Rashford participating in it.

England got to the final of the Euros that summer, where Rashford was one of the players to miss his penalty in the shoot-out against Italy. Ethan had been sad to discover England had lost the next morning, but Monday morning CBeebies went some way to soothing the pain.

A couple of days later, just before bedtime, he'd heard Rashford's name on the TV again and was curious. It wasn't a football game, but the news: a mural paying tribute to

Rashford had been defaced with vile abuse in the aftermath of his missed penalty. In response, hundreds had flocked to the same corner of Withington and plastered the wall with pictures and drawings in support of Rashford.

I was off work the next day so drove us over to see it. We hadn't ended up staying all that long. He was, after all, not yet in primary school by then, and as much as I meant well, as much as I saw this as a chance to teach him something about how good overcomes bad, making a child look at a wall – no matter how impressive – isn't exactly a day at Disneyland.

When I'd buckled him back into his car seat and pulled away from the small car park across the way from the mural, a volley of questions had begun – about Rashford, about how it was possible to play for England if he played for United, about which team had won the most games. Eventually, the conversation had become more United-focused.

'Did you play for United, Daddy?' Ethan asked. I'd laughed and told him how I wasn't very good at football but used to go watching them play with Grandad Dave at Old Trafford. The mention of his name had briefly stemmed the questions.

'Did Grandad Dave take you there in his car?' he started up again.

'Where?'

'That place.'

'Old Trafford? Yeah. It was his favourite place.'

Another pause.

'Where is it?' he asked, inquisitively. 'Could I go there?'

Checking we had the time, I'd asked if he'd like to go and see it right away. And, of course, he did. We left the car on the car park opposite the East Stand and followed the curve of the stadium round to the N42 turnstile which Dad and I had used for much of our final years. Ethan stood in the doorway and I took a picture of him, before we carried on our way.

'Is that Grandad Dave?' he'd asked, catching sight of the statue of Fergie.

'No, that's someone else.'

I'd explained to him that the pitch, the part where the team played, wasn't open on that day. He'd been disappointed at that but I promised him we'd come back another time and watch a game. He bought a new football in the club shop and we'd headed home for some tea.

Ethan's main observation from his brief visit had been that Old Trafford was, just as I'd told him, very big indeed.

Ethan turned five midway through the next football season. By then, United were enduring a train-wreck of a campaign. Ole Gunnar Solskjaer had left after a dismal start to the season and in had come Ralf Rangnick as an interim replacement, failing to spark any revival.

Oblivious to all this, Ethan had steadily been developing an interest since our spontaneous visit to the stadium the previous summer. His attention span didn't allow him to tolerate full 90-minute games yet, but short bursts of match highlights or YouTube compilation videos of Rashford 'doing goals' seemed to grab him for the odd moment.

Trying to manage his burgeoning interest was a delicate process. I'd been tempted to book tickets for Old Trafford for after his birthday in the January but decided against it, not wanting to dampen the enthusiasm which appeared to be growing.

In the end, I'd decided to take him to watch the under-23s play at Leigh Sports Village, which was just around the corner from us. Tickets were free and he'd get a small taste of a football match atmosphere while being able to walk out at half-time if he was too sleepy. In late February, we watched United's youngsters put five goals past Derby County and I was encouraged by how much he'd seemed to enjoy it. Before half-time, he'd joined in with a few tepid chants of 'United' which had risen up from the crowd scattered about in the stand we were sitting in. Emboldened by this, he'd stood up and started to belt out 'Peter Rabbit had a fly upon his nose', which, disappointingly, hadn't quite caught on.

'When are we going to see a game at Old Trafford?' he asked on the drive home.

'Would you like to go soon?' I said, glancing back at him in the rearview mirror.

'Yes.'

That was all the encouragement I'd needed.

* * *

On 2 April 2022 – nearly three years on from my last game – I went back.

As United limped towards the end of a miserable season, they hosted Leicester at home in a match that didn't particularly mean a great deal to anyone – except, perhaps, me.

That morning after breakfast, I'd got Ethan dressed and dug out two United scarves from the back of a cupboard under the stairs: one mine, the other Dad's. We'd set off early, allowing us time for a wander about before the crowds had built up outside the ground.

Leaving the car on the usual car park, I'd tied Dad's scarf loosely around Ethan's neck, held his hand and the pair of us walked the old route to the ground – over the footbridge, up Elevator Road and on to Wharfside Way. After food, we completed a lap of the ground for good luck and passed through the turnstile.

A mate had kindly offered me the tickets and our seats for the day were directly in line with where Dad and I had sat for the final years, but in the tier below. It had been a long time since I'd sat in the lower tier. Being in the older part of the stadium, I'd forgotten how tightly packed the concourse beneath the stand was. It had reminded me of my first games,

Dad pushing me through the crowds with his hands on my shoulders.

I'd accepted by this stage that I'd likely be a blubbering wreck when Ethan ascended the steps and took his first glimpse of the turf. A small part of me hoped he'd be totally underwhelmed by it all, which would have made it easier. The time came. I took out my phone to film the moment and stood a few paces back, allowing him to go up alone as I followed. He reached the top.

'Wooooowwwww!' he beamed, taking in the view. 'It's massive!'

And with that, the tears – big, fat, ugly ones – began to flow. I pulled up my scarf and began to mop them away.

That, I think, was the highlight. The game hadn't been great, with United continuing the season's tradition of looking like a team comprising of players who had only been thrown together that same morning. Leicester had scored first in the second half and it had felt then like that would be it, that Ethan's first game would end in defeat.

Soon after, however, United found an equaliser. Bruno Fernandes worked some space on the edge of the area in front of the Stretford End and aimed a low shot, across Kasper Schmeichel, who managed to get a palm to the ball. Following up had been Fred, who lifted it over him.

Ethan had been tiring by then, asking how much longer it would be that we went home. I'm not entirely sure he saw the ball go in, but when I lifted him up to celebrate it he'd looked slightly alarmed by the noise and clasped his hands over his ears. It wasn't how I'd envisaged our first goal celebration at Old Trafford to be and I'd wondered then if I should have held off a while before bringing him, if he was still a bit too young to have enjoyed it.

The game ended and we waited for a while as the crowds drained out of the exits. When things had quietened down,

I'd taken his hand and led him out, remembering as I did how I'd done that with Dad at his last game.

Away from the stadium, we'd bought a tray of chips from a burger van, smothered them in ketchup and eaten them as we slowly walked back along the quayside towards the car, Ethan tossing a couple in the direction of a swan as we went by.

'Are we going to Old Trafford again soon?' he asked.

'If you want,' I said, smiling.

Perhaps he won't ever take to it, and if so, that's fine. I hope, from a totally selfish perspective, though, that this *is* the start of a new chapter; that despite not wanting to pressurise him into following the same path as me, he decides that yes, that is exactly what he wants to do with his weekends.

Being so hopelessly besotted with a football team undeniably has its downsides. It is a ridiculous concept to those who have never experienced it. But when it is something that's been passed down to you from someone you love, someone who one day won't be around to share it with you, it becomes a difficult thing to shake – even in the bleakest of moments. From my experience, even at the times you *think* you're out for good, I'm not sure you actually can be. Not completely. It's easy to view that as a negative, but when I look at Dad's life now and the relationship between us, there's a comfort to knowing we had something that meant so much to the both of us, that I can go back to Old Trafford whenever I choose and feel that connection to him.

You can be cynical about the general direction in which football appears to be going. But as the sport becomes increasingly infested with greed and threatens to slowly morph into a pissing contest for mega-wealthy, state-owned clubs, there's still something pure about going to a century-old stadium and being able pick out the exact spot where your parents or grandparents stood when they were kids, or the position from where you watched your very first game. To me, that's where the real beauty of being a supporter lies. It isn't strictly about your team being good or bad, but the amalgamation of memories tied to people who mean something to you. For me, that's Dad. In time, maybe it will also be Ethan or Robyn.

For now, I'll wait before I go back to Old Trafford again. When either of them are ready I'll be willing to take them along with me, to tell them all about the history and the tales of the grandad they never knew.

Oh, how much he'd have loved to have come along with us, to be beside us for just one goal.

Acknowledgements

WRITING A book is far harder than I ever imagined it would be, despite how many people attempted to warn me this was the case before I embarked on the journey. Without the people named below, I would have never seen it through. Thank you to all of you.

At Pitch Publishing, Jane Camillin was enthusiastic about me turning my idea into a book from the very first email exchanges. Gareth Davis cast a careful eye over the first draft and was generous with his feedback which, at the end of a long, exhausting process, meant the world.

Stanley Chow produced the brilliant cover image and showed great thoughtfulness in its design after I'd given him a pathetically vague brief over a cup of coffee next to Oxford Road station one Thursday afternoon.

Sophie Steers at Prostate Cancer UK, Naila Ali at Alzheimer's Society and Deborah at Dementia UK were all very helpful in providing me with information for the book relating to Dad's conditions and treatment. Some of the team at Sporting Memories Network, who do wonderful work for those living with dementia, depression or facing isolation and loneliness, also provided invaluable advice. Tony Jameson-Allen was particularly helpful and I intend to one day take him up on his offer of fish and chips in Scarborough.

Several of my former work colleagues were supportive and understanding during the final few months of Dad's

life, namely Matt Stanger, Noz Choudry, Si Clancy, Matt
Sayward, Joe Gilmore, Evan Fanning, Rebecca Fennelly, Ant
D'Angelo, Daniel Orr, Dave Hendry, Jack Sullivan, Steve
Cushnan, Nicky Talent, Wayne Farry, Reuben Pinder, Conor
Cullen, Will Lennard, Swede Mason and Kristian Von Streng
Hæhre. This helped me enormously.

Enda Conway was so keen for me to get back to Old
Trafford and take Ethan along for his first game, he
generously gifted us a couple of free tickets - a gesture I'll
always remember.

Words of encouragement from Babatunde Koiki, Robert
Andrew Powell, Steven Scragg, Karan Tejwani, Wayne
Barton and David Hartrick motivated me during different
stages of the writing process.

I'm also indebted to my circle of close friends – many
of whom I've known since school – for all they've done for
me in recent years and much further back. To Chris Ward,
Richard Brown, Paul Morgan, Daniel Tennent, Danny and
Cal Crompton, Danny Rogers, Ant Stares, Craig Wall,
Michael Murray, Greg Robinson and Jonathan Djabarouti
– cheers, lads.

Most of all, though, thank you to my wife, Lauren. She
has given more to me during the writing of this book than
anyone mentioned above. From tolerating my bad moods to
putting the kids to bed and waiting up until gone midnight
several hundred times to reassure me whatever I'd written
that evening wasn't as terrible as I convinced myself it was.
Love is patient.